History of BBQ

No one is really sure where the term *barbecue* originated. The conventional wisdom is that the Spanish, upon landing in the Caribbean, used the word *barbacoa* to refer to the natives' method of slow-cooking meat over a wooden platform.

By the 19th century, the culinary technique was well established in the American South, and because pigs were prevalent in the region, pork became the primary meat at barbecues.

Barbecue allowed an abundance of food to be cooked at once and quickly became the go-to menu item for large gatherings like church festivals and neighborhood picnics.

Barbecue varies by region, with the four main styles named after their place of origin: **Memphis**; **North Carolina**; **Kansas City**; and **Texas**.

Memphis is renowned for pulled pork-shoulder doused in sweet tomato-based sauce.

North Carolina smokes the whole hog in a vinegar-based sauce.

Kansas City natives prefers ribs cooked in a dry rub, and Texans ... well, Texans dig beef. Eastern Texas' relative proximity to Tennessee puts it in the pulled-pork camp, but in the western segment of the Lone Star State, you're likely to find mesquite-grilled "cowboy-style" brisket.

Locals defend their region's cooking style with the sort of fierce loyalty usually reserved for die-hard sports fans.

However you like to eat your BBQ we can all agree on one thing....

BBQ is a way of LIFE!

"GOOD BARBECUE COMES FROM EXPERIENCE, AND EXPERIENCE, WELL, THAT COMES FROM POOR BARBECUE."
— COUSIN WOODMAN

Barbecue Log Book

Date: [_____]

Meat Type:_____
☐Poultry ☐Pork ☐Beef ☐Seafood ☐Other
Comments:

Weight:_____
Price/lb:_____
☐Fresh ☐ Frozen
Brand/ Store:_____

Meat preparation:

Rub:_____

Glaze:_____

Marinade:_____

Mop Sauce:_____

Cooking procedure:

Cooker used:

Weather/ Conditions:

Target Cooker Temp:_____
Target Wrap Temp:_____
Final Meat Temp:_____
Rest Time length:_____

Fuel used:_____
Qty used:_____

Est Cook Length:_____
Time on:_____ Time off:_____
Actual Cook Length:_____

Wood used:_____
Qty used:_____
☐Logs ☐Chunks ☐Chips
☐Dry ☐Soaked

Comments/ Notes for pre-cook:

Cook Notes:

Post Cook

Date:_____

Post-Cook Evaluation
Rank 1-5 with 5 being Heavenly Perfection, and 1
being Burnt to a Crisp! This allows you to track your cooks.

Exterior Appearance.................   1   2   3   4   5
Comments:_____

Bark Quality............................   1   2   3   4   5
Comments: _____

Smoke Ring.............................   1   2   3   4   5
Comments: _____

Overall Tenderness..................   1   2   3   4   5
Comments: _____

Moisture..................................   1   2   3   4   5
Comments: _____

Aroma.....................................   1   2   3   4   5
Comments: _____

Flavor......................................   1   2   3   4   5
Comments: _____

Other:_____   1   2   3   4   5
Comments: _____

Notes for Next time:

Comments/ Thoughts post-cook:

Barbecue Log Book

Date: _____

Meat Type: _____
☐ Poultry ☐ Pork ☐ Beef ☐ Seafood ☐ Other
Comments:

Weight: _____
Price/lb: _____
☐ Fresh   ☐ Frozen
Brand/ Store: _____

Meat preparation:

Rub: _____

Glaze: _____

Marinade: _____

Mop Sauce: _____

Cooking procedure:

Cooker used:

Weather/ Conditions:

Target Cooker Temp: _____
Target Wrap Temp: _____
Final Meat Temp: _____
Rest Time length: _____

Fuel used: _____
Qty used: _____

Est Cook Length: _____
Time on: _____ Time off: _____
Actual Cook Length: _____

Wood used: _____
Qty used: _____
☐ Logs ☐ Chunks ☐ Chips
☐ Dry ☐ Soaked

Comments/ Notes for pre-cook:

Cook Notes:

Post Cook

Date:_____

Exterior Appearance................   1   2   3   4   5
Comments:_____

Bark Quality............................   1   2   3   4   5
Comments: _____

Smoke Ring............................   1   2   3   4   5
Comments: _____

Overall Tenderness..................   1   2   3   4   5
Comments: _____

Moisture..................................   1   2   3   4   5
Comments: _____

Aroma.....................................   1   2   3   4   5
Comments: _____

Flavor.....................................   1   2   3   4   5
Comments: _____

Other:_____   1   2   3   4   5
Comments: _____

Notes for Next time:

Comments/ Thoughts post-cook:

Barbecue Log Book

Date: _____

Meat Type:_____
☐Poultry ☐Pork ☐Beef ☐Seafood ☐Other
Comments:

Weight:_____
Price/lb:_____
☐Fresh ☐Frozen
Brand/ Store:_____

Meat preparation:

Rub:_____

Glaze:_____

Marinade:_____

Mop Sauce:_____

Cooking procedure:

Cooker used:

Weather/ Conditions:

Target Cooker Temp:_____
Target Wrap Temp:_____
Final Meat Temp:_____
Rest Time length:_____

Est Cook Length:_____
Time on:_____ Time off:_____
Actual Cook Length:_____

Fuel used:_____
Qty used:_____

Wood used:_____
Qty used:_____
☐Logs ☐Chunks ☐Chips
☐Dry ☐Soaked

Comments/ Notes for pre-cook:

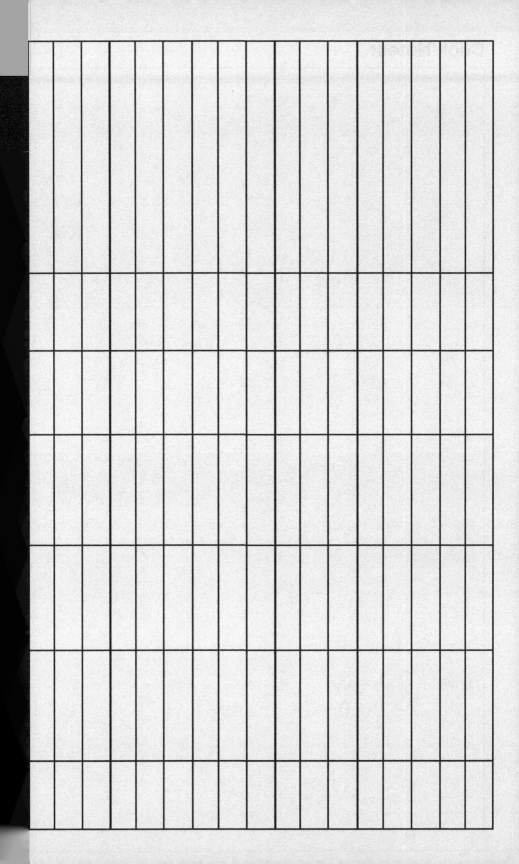

Cook Notes:

Post Cook

Date:_____

Exterior Appearance................   1   2   3   4   5
Comments:_____

Bark Quality............................   1   2   3   4   5
Comments: _____

Smoke Ring............................   1   2   3   4   5
Comments: _____

Overall Tenderness..................   1   2   3   4   5
Comments: _____

Moisture.................................   1   2   3   4   5
Comments: _____

Aroma....................................   1   2   3   4   5
Comments: _____

Flavor....................................   1   2   3   4   5
Comments: _____

Other:_____   1   2   3   4   5
Comments: _____

Notes for Next time:

Comments/ Thoughts post-cook:

Barbecue Log Book

Date: _____

Meat Type:_____
☐Poultry ☐Pork ☐Beef ☐Seafood ☐Other
Comments:

Weight:_____
Price/lb:_____
☐Fresh ☐ Frozen
Brand/ Store:_____

Meat preparation:

Rub:_____

Glaze:_____

Marinade:_____

Mop Sauce:_____

Cooking procedure:

Cooker used:

Weather/ Conditions:

Target Cooker Temp:_____
Target Wrap Temp:_____
Final Meat Temp:_____
Rest Time length:_____

Fuel used:_____
Qty used:_____

Est Cook Length:_____
Time on:_____ Time off:_____
Actual Cook Length:_____

Wood used:_____
Qty used:_____
☐Logs ☐Chunks ☐Chips
☐Dry ☐Soaked

Comments/ Notes for pre-cook:

Cook Notes:

Post Cook

Date:_____

Post-Cook Evaluation
Rank 1-5 with 5 being Heavenly Perfection, and 1
being Burnt to a Crisp! This allows you to track your cooks.

Exterior Appearance................. 1   2   3   4   5
Comments:_____

Bark Quality............................. 1   2   3   4   5
Comments: _____

Smoke Ring............................. 1   2   3   4   5
Comments: _____

Overall Tenderness.................. 1   2   3   4   5
Comments: _____

Moisture................................... 1   2   3   4   5
Comments: _____

Aroma...................................... 1   2   3   4   5
Comments: _____

Flavor...................................... 1   2   3   4   5
Comments: _____

Other:_____ 1   2   3   4   5
Comments: _____

Notes for Next time:

Comments/ Thoughts post-cook:

Barbecue Log Book

Date: _____

Meat Type:_____
☐Poultry ☐Pork ☐Beef ☐Seafood ☐Other
Comments:

Weight:_____
Price/lb:_____
☐Fresh ☐Frozen
Brand/ Store:_____

Meat preparation:

Rub:_____

Glaze:_____

Marinade:_____

Mop Sauce:_____

Cooking procedure:

Cooker used:

Weather/ Conditions:

Target Cooker Temp:_____
Target Wrap Temp:_____
Final Meat Temp:_____
Rest Time length:_____

Fuel used:_____
Qty used:_____

Est Cook Length:_____
Time on:_____ Time off:_____
Actual Cook Length:_____

Wood used:_____
Qty used:_____
☐Logs ☐Chunks ☐Chips
☐Dry ☐Soaked

Comments/ Notes for pre-cook:

Cook Notes:

Post Cook

Date:_____

Post-Cook Evaluation
Rank 1-5 with 5 being Heavenly Perfection, and 1
being Burnt to a Crisp! This allows you to track your cooks.

Exterior Appearance................   1   2   3   4   5
Comments:_____

Bark Quality............................   1   2   3   4   5
Comments: _____

Smoke Ring.............................   1   2   3   4   5
Comments: _____

Overall Tenderness..................   1   2   3   4   5
Comments: _____

Moisture...................................   1   2   3   4   5
Comments: _____

Aroma......................................   1   2   3   4   5
Comments: _____

Flavor......................................   1   2   3   4   5
Comments: _____

Other:_____   1   2   3   4   5
Comments: _____

Notes for Next time:

Comments/ Thoughts post-cook:

Barbecue Log Book

Date: _____

Meat Type:_____
☐Poultry ☐Pork ☐Beef ☐Seafood ☐Other
Comments:

Weight:_____
Price/lb:_____
☐Fresh ☐Frozen
Brand/ Store:_____

Meat preparation:

Rub:_____   Glaze:_____

Marinade:_____   Mop Sauce:_____

Cooking procedure:

Cooker used: Weather/ Conditions:

Target Cooker Temp:_____   Est Cook Length:_____
Target Wrap Temp:_____   Time on:_____ Time off:_____
Final Meat Temp:_____   Actual Cook Length:_____
Rest Time length:_____
                                                          Wood used:_____
Fuel used:_____   Qty used:_____
Qty used:_____   ☐Logs ☐Chunks ☐Chips
                                                          ☐Dry ☐Soaked

Comments/ Notes for pre-cook:

Cook Notes:

Post Cook

Date:_____

Exterior Appearance.................   1   2   3   4   5
Comments:_____

Bark Quality............................   1   2   3   4   5
Comments: _____

Smoke Ring............................   1   2   3   4   5
Comments: _____

Overall Tenderness.................   1   2   3   4   5
Comments: _____

Moisture..................................   1   2   3   4   5
Comments: _____

Aroma.....................................   1   2   3   4   5
Comments: _____

Flavor.....................................   1   2   3   4   5
Comments: _____

Other:_____   1   2   3   4   5
Comments: _____

Notes for Next time:

Comments/ Thoughts post-cook:

Barbecue Log Book

Date: [　　　　　　　]

Meat Type:_____
☐Poultry ☐Pork ☐Beef ☐Seafood ☐Other
Comments:

Weight:_____
Price/lb:_____
☐Fresh ☐Frozen
Brand/ Store:_____

Meat preparation:

Rub:_____

Glaze:_____

Marinade:_____

Mop Sauce:_____

Cooking procedure:

Cooker used:

Weather/ Conditions:

Target Cooker Temp:_____
Target Wrap Temp:_____
Final Meat Temp:_____
Rest Time length:_____

Fuel used:_____
Qty used:_____

Est Cook Length:_____
Time on:_____ Time off:_____
Actual Cook Length:_____

Wood used:_____
Qty used:_____
☐Logs ☐Chunks ☐Chips
☐Dry ☐Soaked

Comments/ Notes for pre-cook:

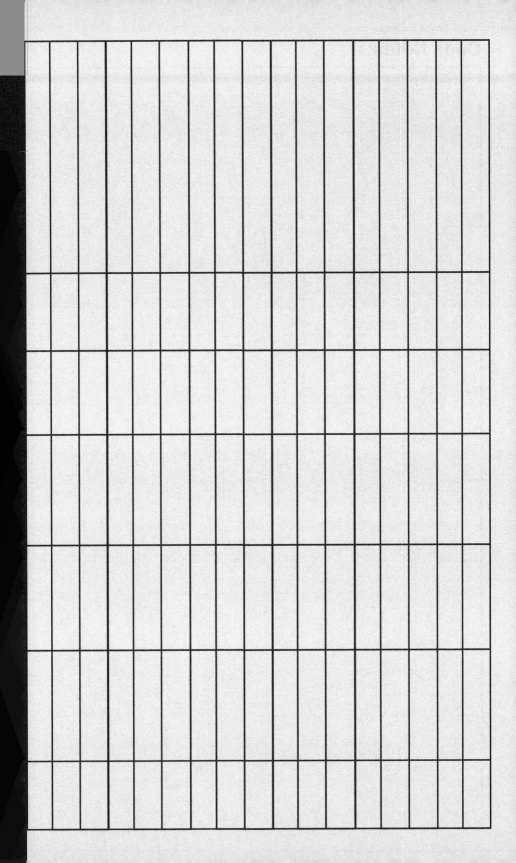

Cook Notes:

Post Cook

Date:_____

Post-Cook Evaluation
Rank 1-5 with 5 being Heavenly Perfection, and 1
being Burnt to a Crisp! This allows you to track your cooks.

Exterior Appearance.................   1   2   3   4   5
Comments:_____

Bark Quality............................   1   2   3   4   5
Comments: _____

Smoke Ring............................   1   2   3   4   5
Comments: _____

Overall Tenderness.................   1   2   3   4   5
Comments: _____

Moisture.................................   1   2   3   4   5
Comments: _____

Aroma....................................   1   2   3   4   5
Comments: _____

Flavor....................................   1   2   3   4   5
Comments: _____

Other:_____   1   2   3   4   5
Comments: _____

Notes for Next time:

Comments/ Thoughts post-cook:

Barbecue Log Book

Date: [＿＿＿＿＿＿]

Meat Type:＿＿＿＿＿＿＿＿
☐Poultry ☐Pork ☐Beef ☐Seafood ☐Other
Comments:

Weight:＿＿＿＿＿＿＿＿＿＿
Price/lb:＿＿＿＿＿＿＿＿＿＿
☐Fresh ☐Frozen
Brand/ Store:＿＿＿＿＿＿＿

Meat preparation:

Rub:＿＿＿＿＿＿＿＿＿＿＿＿
＿＿＿＿＿＿＿＿＿＿＿＿＿＿

Glaze:＿＿＿＿＿＿＿＿＿＿＿
＿＿＿＿＿＿＿＿＿＿＿＿＿＿

Marinade:＿＿＿＿＿＿＿＿＿
＿＿＿＿＿＿＿＿＿＿＿＿＿＿

Mop Sauce:＿＿＿＿＿＿＿＿
＿＿＿＿＿＿＿＿＿＿＿＿＿＿

Cooking procedure:

Cooker used:

Weather/ Conditions:

Target Cooker Temp:＿＿＿＿＿
Target Wrap Temp:＿＿＿＿＿＿
Final Meat Temp:＿＿＿＿＿＿＿
Rest Time length:＿＿＿＿＿＿＿

Fuel used:＿＿＿＿＿＿＿＿＿＿
Qty used:＿＿＿＿＿＿＿＿＿＿＿

Est Cook Length:＿＿＿＿＿＿＿
Time on:＿＿＿＿＿ Time off:＿＿＿＿
Actual Cook Length:＿＿＿＿＿

Wood used:＿＿＿＿＿＿＿＿＿＿
Qty used:＿＿＿＿＿＿＿＿＿＿＿
☐Logs ☐Chunks ☐Chips
☐Dry ☐Soaked

Comments/ Notes for pre-cook:

Cook Notes:

Post Cook

Date:_____

Post-Cook Evaluation
Rank 1-5 with 5 being Heavenly Perfection, and 1
being Burnt to a Crisp! This allows you to track your cooks.

Exterior Appearance.................   1   2   3   4   5
Comments:_____

Bark Quality............................   1   2   3   4   5
Comments: _____

Smoke Ring............................   1   2   3   4   5
Comments: _____

Overall Tenderness.................   1   2   3   4   5
Comments: _____

Moisture..................................   1   2   3   4   5
Comments: _____

Aroma.....................................   1   2   3   4   5
Comments: _____

Flavor.....................................   1   2   3   4   5
Comments: _____

Other:_____   1   2   3   4   5
Comments: _____

Notes for Next time:

Comments/ Thoughts post-cook:

Barbecue Log Book

Date: [_____]

Meat Type:_____
☐Poultry ☐Pork ☐Beef ☐Seafood ☐Other
Comments:

Weight:_____
Price/lb:_____
☐ Fresh   ☐ Frozen
Brand/ Store:_____

Meat preparation:

Rub:_____

Glaze:_____

Marinade:_____

Mop Sauce:_____

Cooking procedure:

Cooker used:

Weather/ Conditions:

Target Cooker Temp:_____
Target Wrap Temp:_____
Final Meat Temp:_____
Rest Time length:_____

Fuel used:_____
Qty used:_____

Est Cook Length:_____
Time on:_____ Time off:_____
Actual Cook Length:_____

Wood used:_____
Qty used:_____
☐Logs ☐Chunks ☐Chips
☐Dry ☐Soaked

Comments/ Notes for pre-cook:

Cook Notes:

Post Cook

Date:_____

Post-Cook Evaluation
Rank 1-5 with 5 being Heavenly Perfection, and 1
being Burnt to a Crisp! This allows you to track your cooks.

Exterior Appearance.................   1   2   3   4   5
Comments:_____

Bark Quality............................   1   2   3   4   5
Comments: _____

Smoke Ring.............................   1   2   3   4   5
Comments: _____

Overall Tenderness.................   1   2   3   4   5
Comments: _____

Moisture...................................   1   2   3   4   5
Comments: _____

Aroma.....................................   1   2   3   4   5
Comments: _____

Flavor.......................................   1   2   3   4   5
Comments: _____

Other:_____   1   2   3   4   5
Comments: _____

Notes for Next time:

Comments/ Thoughts post-cook:

Barbecue Log Book

Date: [_____]

Meat Type:_____
☐Poultry ☐Pork ☐Beef ☐Seafood ☐Other
Comments:

Weight:_____
Price/lb:_____
☐Fresh ☐Frozen
Brand/ Store:_____

Meat preparation:

Rub:_____

Glaze:_____

Marinade:_____

Mop Sauce:_____

Cooking procedure:

Cooker used:

Weather/ Conditions:

Target Cooker Temp:_____
Target Wrap Temp:_____
Final Meat Temp:_____
Rest Time length:_____

Fuel used:_____
Qty used:_____

Est Cook Length:_____
Time on:_____ Time off:_____
Actual Cook Length:_____

Wood used:_____
Qty used:_____
☐Logs ☐Chunks ☐Chips
☐Dry ☐Soaked

Comments/ Notes for pre-cook:

Cook Notes:

Post Cook

Date:_____

Post-Cook Evaluation
Rank 1-5 with 5 being Heavenly Perfection, and 1
being Burnt to a Crisp! This allows you to track your cooks.

Exterior Appearance.................   1   2   3   4   5
Comments:_____

Bark Quality...........................   1   2   3   4   5
Comments: _____

Smoke Ring............................   1   2   3   4   5
Comments: _____

Overall Tenderness..................   1   2   3   4   5
Comments: _____

Moisture...................................   1   2   3   4   5
Comments: _____

Aroma......................................   1   2   3   4   5
Comments: _____

Flavor......................................   1   2   3   4   5
Comments: _____

Other:_____   1   2   3   4   5
Comments: _____

Notes for Next time:

Comments/ Thoughts post-cook:

Barbecue Log Book

Date: _____

Meat Type:_____
☐Poultry ☐Pork ☐Beef ☐Seafood ☐Other
Comments:

Weight:_____
Price/lb:_____
☐ Fresh   ☐ Frozen
Brand/ Store:_____

Meat preparation:

Rub:_____

Glaze:_____

Marinade:_____

Mop Sauce:_____

Cooking procedure:

Cooker used:

Weather/ Conditions:

Target Cooker Temp:_____
Target Wrap Temp:_____
Final Meat Temp:_____
Rest Time length:_____

Fuel used:_____
Qty used:_____

Est Cook Length:_____
Time on:_____ Time off:_____
Actual Cook Length:_____

Wood used:_____
Qty used:_____
☐Logs ☐Chunks ☐Chips
☐Dry ☐Soaked

Comments/ Notes for pre-cook:

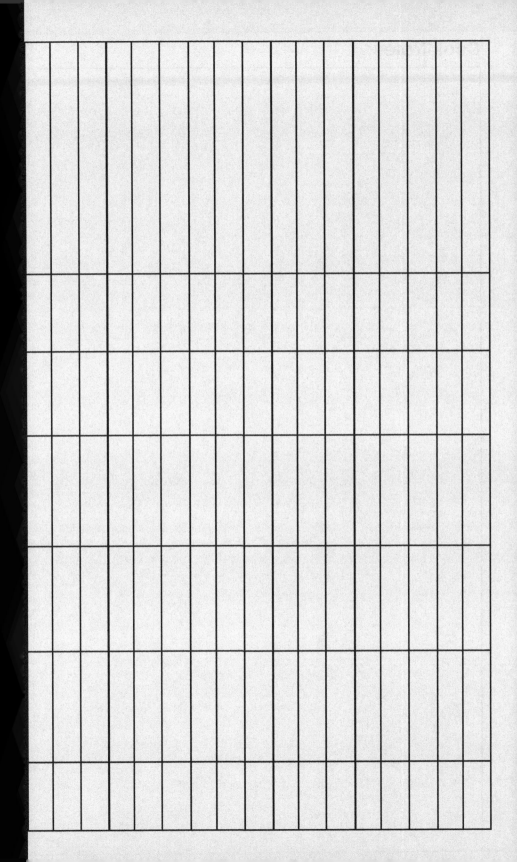

Cook Notes:

Post Cook

Date:_____

Post-Cook Evaluation
Rank 1-5 with 5 being Heavenly Perfection, and 1
being Burnt to a Crisp! This allows you to track your cooks.

Exterior Appearance.............. 1   2   3   4   5
Comments:_____

Bark Quality............................ 1   2   3   4   5
Comments: _____

Smoke Ring........................... 1   2   3   4   5
Comments: _____

Overall Tenderness................. 1   2   3   4   5
Comments: _____

Moisture................................... 1   2   3   4   5
Comments: _____

Aroma..................................... 1   2   3   4   5
Comments: _____

Flavor...................................... 1   2   3   4   5
Comments: _____

Other:_____ 1   2   3   4   5
Comments: _____

Notes for Next time:

Comments/ Thoughts post-cook:

Barbecue Log Book

Date: _____

Meat Type:_____
☐Poultry ☐Pork ☐Beef ☐Seafood ☐Other
Comments:

Weight:_____
Price/lb:_____
☐Fresh ☐Frozen
Brand/ Store:_____

Meat preparation:

Rub:_____ Glaze:_____
_____ _____

Marinade:_____ Mop Sauce:_____
_____ _____

Cooking procedure:

Cooker used:

Weather/ Conditions:

Target Cooker Temp:_____
Target Wrap Temp:_____
Final Meat Temp:_____
Rest Time length:_____

Fuel used:_____
Qty used:_____

Est Cook Length:_____
Time on:_____ Time off:_____
Actual Cook Length:_____

Wood used:_____
Qty used:_____
☐Logs ☐Chunks ☐Chips
☐Dry ☐Soaked

Comments/ Notes for pre-cook:

Cook Notes:

Post Cook

Date:_____

Post-Cook Evaluation
Rank 1-5 with 5 being Heavenly Perfection, and 1
being Burnt to a Crisp! This allows you to track your cooks.

Exterior Appearance.................   1   2   3   4   5
Comments:_____

Bark Quality............................   1   2   3   4   5
Comments: _____

Smoke Ring.............................   1   2   3   4   5
Comments: _____

Overall Tenderness..................   1   2   3   4   5
Comments: _____

Moisture..................................   1   2   3   4   5
Comments: _____

Aroma.....................................   1   2   3   4   5
Comments: _____

Flavor......................................   1   2   3   4   5
Comments: _____

Other:_____   1   2   3   4   5
Comments: _____

Notes for Next time:

Comments/ Thoughts post-cook:

Barbecue Log Book

Date: [_____]

Meat Type:_____
☐Poultry ☐Pork ☐Beef ☐Seafood ☐Other
Comments:

Weight:_____
Price/lb:_____
☐Fresh   ☐Frozen
Brand/ Store:_____

Meat preparation:

Rub:_____

Glaze:_____

Marinade:_____

Mop Sauce:_____

Cooking procedure:

Cooker used:

Weather/ Conditions:

Target Cooker Temp:_____
Target Wrap Temp:_____
Final Meat Temp:_____
Rest Time length:_____

Fuel used:_____
Qty used:_____

Est Cook Length:_____
Time on:_____ Time off:_____
Actual Cook Length:_____

Wood used:_____
Qty used:_____
☐Logs ☐Chunks ☐Chips
☐Dry ☐Soaked

Comments/ Notes for pre-cook:

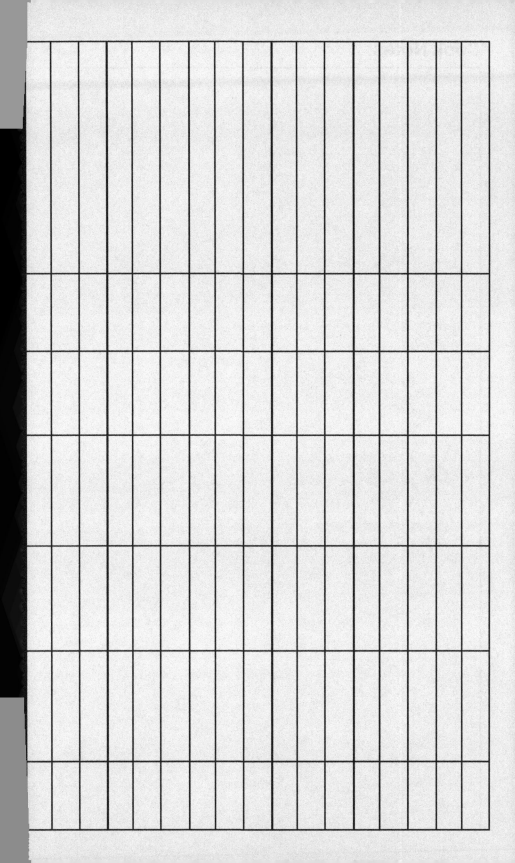

Cook Notes:

Post Cook

Date:_____

Post-Cook Evaluation
Rank 1-5 with 5 being Heavenly Perfection, and 1
being Burnt to a Crisp! This allows you to track your cooks.

Exterior Appearance.................   1   2   3   4   5
Comments:_____

Bark Quality...........................   1   2   3   4   5
Comments: _____

Smoke Ring............................   1   2   3   4   5
Comments: _____

Overall Tenderness.................   1   2   3   4   5
Comments: _____

Moisture.................................   1   2   3   4   5
Comments: _____

Aroma....................................   1   2   3   4   5
Comments: _____

Flavor....................................   1   2   3   4   5
Comments: _____

Other:_____   1   2   3   4   5
Comments: _____

Notes for Next time:

Comments/ Thoughts post-cook:

Barbecue Log Book

Date: [ ]

Meat Type:_____
☐Poultry ☐Pork ☐Beef ☐Seafood ☐Other
Comments:

Weight:_____
Price/lb:_____
☐Fresh ☐ Frozen
Brand/ Store:_____

Meat preparation:

Rub:_____

Glaze:_____

Marinade:_____

Mop Sauce:_____

Cooking procedure:

Cooker used:

Weather/ Conditions:

Target Cooker Temp:_____
Target Wrap Temp:_____
Final Meat Temp:_____
Rest Time length:_____

Fuel used:_____
Qty used:_____

Est Cook Length:_____
Time on:_____ Time off:_____
Actual Cook Length:_____

Wood used:_____
Qty used:_____
☐Logs ☐Chunks ☐Chips
☐Dry ☐Soaked

Comments/ Notes for pre-cook:

Cook Notes:

Post Cook

Date:_____

Post-Cook Evaluation
Rank 1-5 with 5 being Heavenly Perfection, and 1
being Burnt to a Crisp! This allows you to track your cooks.

Exterior Appearance................   1   2   3   4   5
Comments:_____

Bark Quality...........................   1   2   3   4   5
Comments: _____

Smoke Ring...........................   1   2   3   4   5
Comments: _____

Overall Tenderness.................   1   2   3   4   5
Comments: _____

Moisture.................................   1   2   3   4   5
Comments: _____

Aroma...................................   1   2   3   4   5
Comments: _____

Flavor....................................   1   2   3   4   5
Comments: _____

Other:_____   1   2   3   4   5
Comments: _____

Notes for Next time:

Comments/ Thoughts post-cook:

Barbecue Log Book

Date: [_____]

Meat Type:_____
☐Poultry ☐Pork ☐Beef ☐Seafood ☐Other
Comments:

Weight:_____
Price/lb:_____
☐ Fresh   ☐ Frozen
Brand/ Store:_____

Meat preparation:

Rub:_____

Glaze:_____

Marinade:_____

Mop Sauce:_____

Cooking procedure:

Cooker used:

Weather/ Conditions:

Target Cooker Temp:_____
Target Wrap Temp:_____
Final Meat Temp:_____
Rest Time length:_____

Fuel used:_____
Qty used:_____

Est Cook Length:_____
Time on:_____ Time off:_____
Actual Cook Length:_____

Wood used:_____
Qty used:_____
☐Logs ☐Chunks ☐Chips
☐Dry ☐Soaked

Comments/ Notes for pre-cook:

Cook Notes:

Post Cook

Date:_____

Post-Cook Evaluation
Rank 1-5 with 5 being Heavenly Perfection, and 1
being Burnt to a Crisp! This allows you to track your cooks.

Exterior Appearance................   1   2   3   4   5
Comments:_____

Bark Quality...........................   1   2   3   4   5
Comments: _____

Smoke Ring............................   1   2   3   4   5
Comments: _____

Overall Tenderness.................   1   2   3   4   5
Comments: _____

Moisture.................................   1   2   3   4   5
Comments: _____

Aroma....................................   1   2   3   4   5
Comments: _____

Flavor.....................................   1   2   3   4   5
Comments: _____

Other:_____   1   2   3   4   5
Comments: _____

Notes for Next time:

Comments/ Thoughts post-cook:

Barbecue Log Book

Date: _____

Meat Type:_____
☐Poultry ☐Pork ☐Beef ☐Seafood ☐Other
Comments:

Weight:_____
Price/lb:_____
☐Fresh ☐Frozen
Brand/ Store:_____

Meat preparation:

Rub:_____

Glaze:_____

Marinade:_____

Mop Sauce:_____

Cooking procedure:

Cooker used:

Weather/ Conditions:

Target Cooker Temp:_____
Target Wrap Temp:_____
Final Meat Temp:_____
Rest Time length:_____

Fuel used:_____
Qty used:_____

Est Cook Length:_____
Time on:_____ Time off:_____
Actual Cook Length:_____

Wood used:_____
Qty used:_____
☐Logs ☐Chunks ☐Chips
☐Dry ☐Soaked

Comments/ Notes for pre-cook:

Cook Notes:

Post Cook

Date:_____

Post-Cook Evaluation
Rank 1-5 with 5 being Heavenly Perfection, and 1
being Burnt to a Crisp! This allows you to track your cooks.

Exterior Appearance................ 1   2   3   4   5
Comments:_____

Bark Quality............................ 1   2   3   4   5
Comments: _____

Smoke Ring............................. 1   2   3   4   5
Comments: _____

Overall Tenderness.................. 1   2   3   4   5
Comments: _____

Moisture.................................. 1   2   3   4   5
Comments: _____

Aroma..................................... 1   2   3   4   5
Comments: _____

Flavor...................................... 1   2   3   4   5
Comments: _____

Other:_____ 1   2   3   4   5
Comments: _____

Notes for Next time:

Comments/ Thoughts post-cook:

Barbecue Log Book

Date: _____

Meat Type: _____
☐Poultry ☐Pork ☐Beef ☐Seafood ☐Other
Comments:

Weight: _____
Price/lb: _____
☐Fresh ☐ Frozen
Brand/ Store: _____

Meat preparation:

Rub: _____

Glaze: _____

Marinade: _____

Mop Sauce: _____

Cooking procedure:

Cooker used:

Weather/ Conditions:

Target Cooker Temp: _____
Target Wrap Temp: _____
Final Meat Temp: _____
Rest Time length: _____

Fuel used: _____
Qty used: _____

Est Cook Length: _____
Time on: _____ Time off: _____
Actual Cook Length: _____

Wood used: _____
Qty used: _____
☐Logs ☐Chunks ☐Chips
☐Dry ☐Soaked

Comments/ Notes for pre-cook:

Cook Notes:

Post Cook

Date:_____

Post-Cook Evaluation
Rank 1-5 with 5 being Heavenly Perfection, and 1
being Burnt to a Crisp! This allows you to track your cooks.

Exterior Appearance................   1   2   3   4   5
Comments:_____

Bark Quality............................   1   2   3   4   5
Comments: _____

Smoke Ring............................   1   2   3   4   5
Comments: _____

Overall Tenderness.................   1   2   3   4   5
Comments: _____

Moisture.................................   1   2   3   4   5
Comments: _____

Aroma....................................   1   2   3   4   5
Comments: _____

Flavor.....................................   1   2   3   4   5
Comments: _____

Other:_____   1   2   3   4   5
Comments: _____

Notes for Next time:

Comments/ Thoughts post-cook:

Barbecue Log Book

Date: _____

Meat Type:_____
☐Poultry ☐Pork ☐Beef ☐Seafood ☐Other
Comments:

Weight:_____
Price/lb:_____
☐Fresh ☐Frozen
Brand/ Store:_____

Meat preparation:

Rub:_____

Glaze:_____

Marinade:_____

Mop Sauce:_____

Cooking procedure:

Cooker used:

Weather/ Conditions:

Target Cooker Temp:_____
Target Wrap Temp:_____
Final Meat Temp:_____
Rest Time length:_____

Fuel used:_____
Qty used:_____

Est Cook Length:_____
Time on:_____ Time off:_____
Actual Cook Length:_____

Wood used:_____
Qty used:_____
☐Logs ☐Chunks ☐Chips
☐Dry ☐Soaked

Comments/ Notes for pre-cook:

Cook Notes:

Post Cook

Date:_____

Exterior Appearance................   1   2   3   4   5
Comments:_____

Bark Quality............................   1   2   3   4   5
Comments: _____

Smoke Ring.............................   1   2   3   4   5
Comments: _____

Overall Tenderness..................   1   2   3   4   5
Comments: _____

Moisture...................................   1   2   3   4   5
Comments: _____

Aroma......................................   1   2   3   4   5
Comments: _____

Flavor......................................   1   2   3   4   5
Comments: _____

Other:_____   1   2   3   4   5
Comments: _____

Notes for Next time:

Comments/ Thoughts post-cook:

Barbecue Log Book

Date: _____

Meat Type:_____
☐Poultry ☐Pork ☐Beef ☐Seafood ☐Other
Comments:

Weight:_____
Price/lb:_____
☐Fresh ☐Frozen
Brand/ Store:_____

Meat preparation:

Rub:_____

Glaze:_____

Marinade:_____

Mop Sauce:_____

Cooking procedure:

Cooker used:

Weather/ Conditions:

Target Cooker Temp:_____
Target Wrap Temp:_____
Final Meat Temp:_____
Rest Time length:_____

Fuel used:_____
Qty used:_____

Est Cook Length:_____
Time on:_____ Time off:_____
Actual Cook Length:_____

Wood used:_____
Qty used:_____
☐Logs ☐Chunks ☐Chips
☐Dry ☐Soaked

Comments/ Notes for pre-cook:

Cook Notes:

Post Cook

Date:_____

Post-Cook Evaluation
Rank 1-5 with 5 being Heavenly Perfection, and 1
being Burnt to a Crisp! This allows you to track your cooks.

Exterior Appearance................   1   2   3   4   5
Comments:_____

Bark Quality............................   1   2   3   4   5
Comments: _____

Smoke Ring.............................   1   2   3   4   5
Comments: _____

Overall Tenderness..................   1   2   3   4   5
Comments: _____

Moisture...................................   1   2   3   4   5
Comments: _____

Aroma......................................   1   2   3   4   5
Comments: _____

Flavor......................................   1   2   3   4   5
Comments: _____

Other:_____   1   2   3   4   5
Comments: _____

Notes for Next time:

Comments/ Thoughts post-cook:

Barbecue Log Book

Date: _____

Meat Type:_____
☐Poultry ☐Pork ☐Beef ☐Seafood ☐Other
Comments:

Weight:_____
Price/lb:_____
☐Fresh ☐Frozen
Brand/ Store:_____

Meat preparation:

Rub:_____

Glaze:_____

Marinade:_____

Mop Sauce:_____

Cooking procedure:

Cooker used:

Weather/ Conditions:

Target Cooker Temp:_____
Target Wrap Temp:_____
Final Meat Temp:_____
Rest Time length:_____

Fuel used:_____
Qty used:_____

Est Cook Length:_____
Time on:_____ Time off:_____
Actual Cook Length:_____

Wood used:_____
Qty used:_____
☐Logs ☐Chunks ☐Chips
☐Dry ☐Soaked

Comments/ Notes for pre-cook:

Cook Notes:

Post Cook

Date:_____

Post-Cook Evaluation
Rank 1-5 with 5 being Heavenly Perfection, and 1
being Burnt to a Crisp! This allows you to track your cooks.

Exterior Appearance................. 1   2   3   4   5
Comments:_____

Bark Quality............................ 1   2   3   4   5
Comments: _____

Smoke Ring............................. 1   2   3   4   5
Comments: _____

Overall Tenderness.................. 1   2   3   4   5
Comments: _____

Moisture.................................. 1   2   3   4   5
Comments: _____

Aroma...................................... 1   2   3   4   5
Comments: _____

Flavor...................................... 1   2   3   4   5
Comments: _____

Other:_____ 1   2   3   4   5
Comments: _____

Notes for Next time:

Comments/ Thoughts post-cook:

Barbecue Log Book

Date: _____

Meat Type:_____
☐Poultry ☐Pork ☐Beef ☐Seafood ☐Other
Comments:

Weight:_____
Price/lb:_____
☐Fresh   ☐Frozen
Brand/ Store:_____

Meat preparation:

Rub:_____

Glaze:_____

Marinade:_____

Mop Sauce:_____

Cooking procedure:

Cooker used:

Weather/ Conditions:

Target Cooker Temp:_____
Target Wrap Temp:_____
Final Meat Temp:_____
Rest Time length:_____

Fuel used:_____
Qty used:_____

Est Cook Length:_____
Time on:_____ Time off:_____
Actual Cook Length:_____

Wood used:_____
Qty used:_____
☐Logs ☐Chunks ☐Chips
☐Dry ☐Soaked

Comments/ Notes for pre-cook:

Cook Notes:

Post Cook

Date:_____

Exterior Appearance................   1   2   3   4   5
Comments:_____

Bark Quality............................   1   2   3   4   5
Comments: _____

Smoke Ring............................   1   2   3   4   5
Comments: _____

Overall Tenderness.................   1   2   3   4   5
Comments: _____

Moisture..................................   1   2   3   4   5
Comments: _____

Aroma.....................................   1   2   3   4   5
Comments: _____

Flavor.....................................   1   2   3   4   5
Comments: _____

Other:_____   1   2   3   4   5
Comments: _____

Notes for Next time:

Comments/ Thoughts post-cook:

Barbecue Log Book

Date: _____

Meat Type:_____
☐Poultry ☐Pork ☐Beef ☐Seafood ☐Other
Comments:

Weight:_____
Price/lb:_____
☐ Fresh   ☐ Frozen
Brand/ Store:_____

Meat preparation:

Rub:_____

Glaze:_____

Marinade:_____

Mop Sauce:_____

Cooking procedure:

Cooker used:

Weather/ Conditions:

Target Cooker Temp:_____
Target Wrap Temp:_____
Final Meat Temp:_____
Rest Time length:_____

Fuel used:_____
Qty used:_____

Est Cook Length:_____
Time on:_____ Time off:_____
Actual Cook Length:_____

Wood used:_____
Qty used:_____
☐Logs ☐Chunks ☐Chips
☐Dry ☐Soaked

Comments/ Notes for pre-cook:

Cook Notes:

Post Cook

Date:_____

Exterior Appearance................   1   2   3   4   5
Comments:_____

Bark Quality...........................   1   2   3   4   5
Comments: _____

Smoke Ring............................   1   2   3   4   5
Comments: _____

Overall Tenderness.................   1   2   3   4   5
Comments: _____

Moisture..................................   1   2   3   4   5
Comments: _____

Aroma.....................................   1   2   3   4   5
Comments: _____

Flavor.....................................   1   2   3   4   5
Comments: _____

Other:_____   1   2   3   4   5
Comments: _____

Notes for Next time:

Comments/ Thoughts post-cook:

Barbecue Log Book

Date: _____

Meat Type:_____
☐Poultry ☐Pork ☐Beef ☐Seafood ☐Other
Comments:

Weight:_____
Price/lb:_____
☐Fresh   ☐Frozen
Brand/ Store:_____

Meat preparation:

Rub:_____

Glaze:_____
_____

Marinade:_____

Mop Sauce:_____
_____

Cooking procedure:

Cooker used:

Weather/ Conditions:

Target Cooker Temp:_____
Target Wrap Temp:_____
Final Meat Temp:_____
Rest Time length:_____

Fuel used:_____
Qty used:_____

Est Cook Length:_____
Time on:_____ Time off:_____
Actual Cook Length:_____

Wood used:_____
Qty used:_____
☐Logs ☐Chunks ☐Chips
☐Dry ☐Soaked

Comments/ Notes for pre-cook:

Cook Notes:

Post Cook

Date:_____

Post-Cook Evaluation
Rank 1-5 with 5 being Heavenly Perfection, and 1
being Burnt to a Crisp! This allows you to track your cooks.

Exterior Appearance................   1   2   3   4   5
Comments:_____

Bark Quality...........................   1   2   3   4   5
Comments: _____

Smoke Ring...........................   1   2   3   4   5
Comments: _____

Overall Tenderness................   1   2   3   4   5
Comments: _____

Moisture.................................   1   2   3   4   5
Comments: _____

Aroma....................................   1   2   3   4   5
Comments: _____

Flavor....................................   1   2   3   4   5
Comments: _____

Other:_____   1   2   3   4   5
Comments: _____

Notes for Next time:

Comments/ Thoughts post-cook:

Barbecue Log Book

Date: [_____]

Meat Type:_____
☐Poultry ☐Pork ☐Beef ☐Seafood ☐Other
Comments:

Weight:_____
Price/lb:_____
☐Fresh   ☐Frozen
Brand/ Store:_____

Meat preparation:

Rub:_____

Glaze:_____

Marinade:_____

Mop Sauce:_____

Cooking procedure:

Cooker used:

Weather/ Conditions:

Target Cooker Temp:_____
Target Wrap Temp:_____
Final Meat Temp:_____
Rest Time length:_____

Fuel used:_____
Qty used:_____

Est Cook Length:_____
Time on:_____ Time off:_____
Actual Cook Length:_____

Wood used:_____
Qty used:_____
☐Logs ☐Chunks ☐Chips
☐Dry ☐Soaked

Comments/ Notes for pre-cook:

Cook Notes:

Post Cook

Date:_____

Post-Cook Evaluation
Rank 1-5 with 5 being Heavenly Perfection, and 1
being Burnt to a Crisp! This allows you to track your cooks.

Exterior Appearance................. 1   2   3   4   5
Comments:_____

Bark Quality............................ 1   2   3   4   5
Comments: _____

Smoke Ring............................. 1   2   3   4   5
Comments: _____

Overall Tenderness.................. 1   2   3   4   5
Comments: _____

Moisture.................................. 1   2   3   4   5
Comments: _____

Aroma..................................... 1   2   3   4   5
Comments: _____

Flavor...................................... 1   2   3   4   5
Comments: _____

Other:_____ 1   2   3   4   5
Comments: _____

Notes for Next time:

Comments/ Thoughts post-cook:

Barbecue Log Book

Date: [_____]

Meat Type:_____
☐Poultry ☐Pork ☐Beef ☐Seafood ☐Other
Comments:

Weight:_____
Price/lb:_____
☐Fresh ☐Frozen
Brand/ Store:_____

Meat preparation:

Rub:_____

Glaze:_____
_____

Marinade:_____

Mop Sauce:_____
_____

Cooking procedure:

Cooker used:

Weather/ Conditions:

Target Cooker Temp:_____
Target Wrap Temp:_____
Final Meat Temp:_____
Rest Time length:_____

Fuel used:_____
Qty used:_____

Est Cook Length:_____
Time on:_____ Time off:_____
Actual Cook Length:_____

Wood used:_____
Qty used:_____
☐Logs ☐Chunks ☐Chips
☐Dry ☐Soaked

Comments/ Notes for pre-cook:

Cook Notes:

Post Cook

Date:_____

Post-Cook Evaluation
Rank 1-5 with 5 being Heavenly Perfection, and 1
being Burnt to a Crisp! This allows you to track your cooks.

Exterior Appearance.................   1   2   3   4   5
Comments:_____

Bark Quality............................   1   2   3   4   5
Comments: _____

Smoke Ring.............................   1   2   3   4   5
Comments: _____

Overall Tenderness..................   1   2   3   4   5
Comments: _____

Moisture..................................   1   2   3   4   5
Comments: _____

Aroma.....................................   1   2   3   4   5
Comments: _____

Flavor.......................................   1   2   3   4   5
Comments: _____

Other:_____   1   2   3   4   5
Comments: _____

Notes for Next time:

Comments/ Thoughts post-cook:

Barbecue Log Book

Date: [   ]

Meat Type:_____
☐Poultry ☐Pork ☐Beef ☐Seafood ☐Other
Comments:

Weight:_____
Price/lb:_____
☐Fresh ☐Frozen
Brand/ Store:_____

Meat preparation:

Rub:_____

Glaze:_____

Marinade:_____

Mop Sauce:_____

Cooking procedure:

Cooker used:

Weather/ Conditions:

Target Cooker Temp:_____
Target Wrap Temp:_____
Final Meat Temp:_____
Rest Time length:_____

Fuel used:_____
Qty used:_____

Est Cook Length:_____
Time on:_____ Time off:_____
Actual Cook Length:_____

Wood used:_____
Qty used:_____
☐Logs ☐Chunks ☐Chips
☐Dry ☐Soaked

Comments/ Notes for pre-cook:

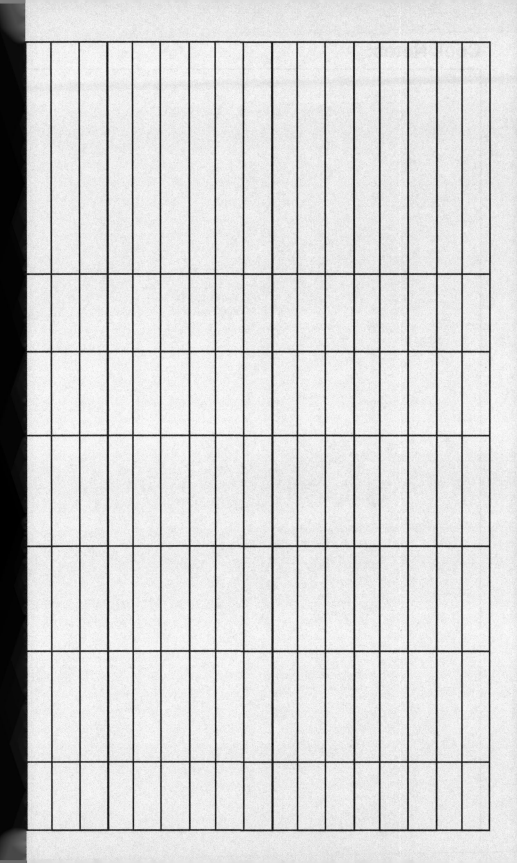

Cook Notes:

Post Cook

Date:_____

Post-Cook Evaluation
Rank 1-5 with 5 being Heavenly Perfection, and 1
being Burnt to a Crisp! This allows you to track your cooks.

Exterior Appearance................   1   2   3   4   5
Comments:_____

Bark Quality............................   1   2   3   4   5
Comments: _____

Smoke Ring.............................   1   2   3   4   5
Comments: _____

Overall Tenderness..................   1   2   3   4   5
Comments: _____

Moisture...................................   1   2   3   4   5
Comments: _____

Aroma......................................   1   2   3   4   5
Comments: _____

Flavor......................................   1   2   3   4   5
Comments: _____

Other:_____   1   2   3   4   5
Comments: _____

Notes for Next time:

Comments/ Thoughts post-cook:

Barbecue Log Book

Date: [_____]

Meat Type:_____
☐Poultry ☐Pork ☐Beef ☐Seafood ☐Other
Comments:

Weight:_____
Price/lb:_____
☐Fresh ☐ Frozen
Brand/ Store:_____

Meat preparation:

Rub:_____

Glaze:_____

Marinade:_____

Mop Sauce:_____

Cooking procedure:

Cooker used:

Weather/ Conditions:

Target Cooker Temp:_____
Target Wrap Temp:_____
Final Meat Temp:_____
Rest Time length:_____

Fuel used:_____
Qty used:_____

Est Cook Length:_____
Time on:_____ Time off:_____
Actual Cook Length:_____

Wood used:_____
Qty used:_____
☐Logs ☐Chunks ☐Chips
☐Dry ☐Soaked

Comments/ Notes for pre-cook:

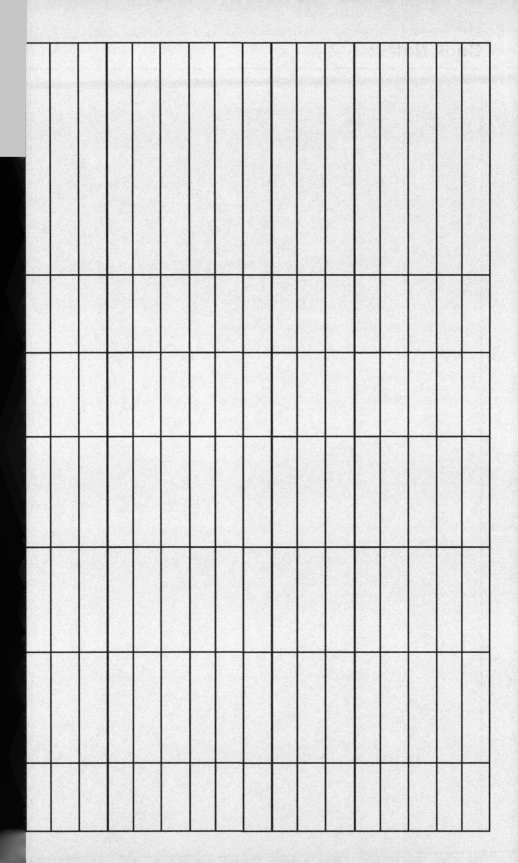

Cook Notes:

Post Cook

Date:_____

Post-Cook Evaluation
Rank 1-5 with 5 being Heavenly Perfection, and 1
being Burnt to a Crisp! This allows you to track your cooks.

Exterior Appearance................. 1   2   3   4   5
Comments:_____

Bark Quality............................ 1   2   3   4   5
Comments: _____

Smoke Ring............................ 1   2   3   4   5
Comments: _____

Overall Tenderness................. 1   2   3   4   5
Comments: _____

Moisture................................... 1   2   3   4   5
Comments: _____

Aroma..................................... 1   2   3   4   5
Comments: _____

Flavor...................................... 1   2   3   4   5
Comments: _____

Other:_____ 1   2   3   4   5
Comments: _____

Notes for Next time:

Comments/ Thoughts post-cook:

Barbecue Log Book

Date: _____

Meat Type:_____
☐Poultry ☐Pork ☐Beef ☐Seafood ☐Other
Comments:

Weight:_____
Price/lb:_____
☐Fresh ☐Frozen
Brand/ Store:_____

Meat preparation:

Rub:_____
_____

Glaze:_____
_____

Marinade:_____
_____

Mop Sauce:_____
_____

Cooking procedure:

Cooker used:

Weather/ Conditions:

Target Cooker Temp:_____
Target Wrap Temp:_____
Final Meat Temp:_____
Rest Time length:_____

Fuel used:_____
Qty used:_____

Est Cook Length:_____
Time on:_____ Time off:_____
Actual Cook Length:_____

Wood used:_____
Qty used:_____
☐Logs ☐Chunks ☐Chips
☐Dry ☐Soaked

Comments/ Notes for pre-cook:

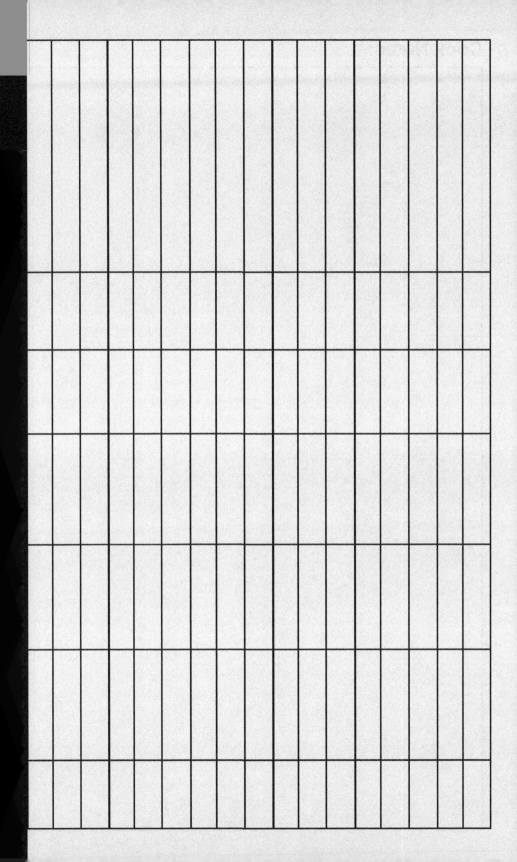

Cook Notes:

Post Cook

Date:_____

Post-Cook Evaluation
Rank 1-5 with 5 being Heavenly Perfection, and 1
being Burnt to a Crisp! This allows you to track your cooks.

Exterior Appearance................   1   2   3   4   5
Comments:_____

Bark Quality............................   1   2   3   4   5
Comments: _____

Smoke Ring............................   1   2   3   4   5
Comments: _____

Overall Tenderness.................   1   2   3   4   5
Comments: _____

Moisture.................................   1   2   3   4   5
Comments: _____

Aroma....................................   1   2   3   4   5
Comments: _____

Flavor.....................................   1   2   3   4   5
Comments: _____

Other:_____   1   2   3   4   5
Comments: _____

Notes for Next time:

Comments/ Thoughts post-cook:

Barbecue Log Book

Date: _____

Meat Type:_____
☐Poultry ☐Pork ☐Beef ☐Seafood ☐Other
Comments:

Weight:_____
Price/lb:_____
☐Fresh ☐Frozen
Brand/ Store:_____

Meat preparation:

Rub:_____

Glaze:_____

Marinade:_____

Mop Sauce:_____

Cooking procedure:

Cooker used:

Weather/ Conditions:

Target Cooker Temp:_____
Target Wrap Temp:_____
Final Meat Temp:_____
Rest Time length:_____

Est Cook Length:_____
Time on:_____ Time off:_____
Actual Cook Length:_____

Fuel used:_____
Qty used:_____

Wood used:_____
Qty used:_____
☐Logs ☐Chunks ☐Chips
☐Dry ☐Soaked

Comments/ Notes for pre-cook:

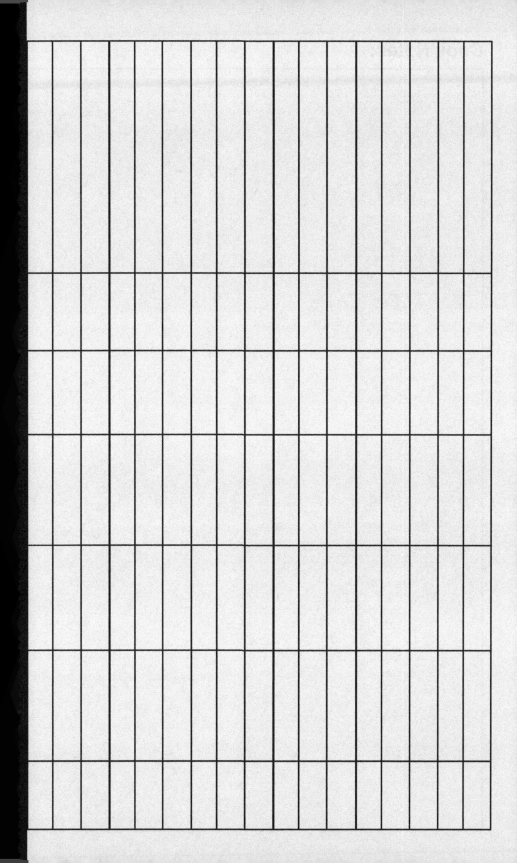

Cook Notes:

Post Cook

Date:_____

Post-Cook Evaluation
Rank 1-5 with 5 being Heavenly Perfection, and 1
being Burnt to a Crisp! This allows you to track your cooks.

Exterior Appearance................   1   2   3   4   5
Comments:_____

Bark Quality.............................   1   2   3   4   5
Comments: _____

Smoke Ring.............................   1   2   3   4   5
Comments: _____

Overall Tenderness..................   1   2   3   4   5
Comments: _____

Moisture..................................   1   2   3   4   5
Comments: _____

Aroma.....................................   1   2   3   4   5
Comments: _____

Flavor.......................................   1   2   3   4   5
Comments: _____

Other:_____   1   2   3   4   5
Comments: _____

Notes for Next time:

Comments/ Thoughts post-cook:

Barbecue Log Book

Date: [_____]

Meat Type:_____
☐Poultry ☐Pork ☐Beef ☐Seafood ☐Other
Comments:

Weight:_____
Price/lb:_____
☐ Fresh   ☐ Frozen
Brand/ Store:_____

Meat preparation:

Rub:_____
_____

Glaze:_____
_____

Marinade:_____
_____

Mop Sauce:_____
_____

Cooking procedure:

Cooker used:

Weather/ Conditions:

Target Cooker Temp:_____
Target Wrap Temp:_____
Final Meat Temp:_____
Rest Time length:_____

Fuel used:_____
Qty used:_____

Est Cook Length:_____
Time on:_____ Time off:_____
Actual Cook Length:_____

Wood used:_____
Qty used:_____
☐Logs ☐Chunks ☐Chips
☐Dry ☐Soaked

Comments/ Notes for pre-cook:

Cook Notes:

Post Cook

Date:_____

Post-Cook Evaluation
Rank 1-5 with 5 being Heavenly Perfection, and 1
being Burnt to a Crisp! This allows you to track your cooks.

Exterior Appearance................   1   2   3   4   5
Comments:_____

Bark Quality............................   1   2   3   4   5
Comments: _____

Smoke Ring............................   1   2   3   4   5
Comments: _____

Overall Tenderness.................   1   2   3   4   5
Comments: _____

Moisture...................................   1   2   3   4   5
Comments: _____

Aroma......................................   1   2   3   4   5
Comments: _____

Flavor......................................   1   2   3   4   5
Comments: _____

Other:_____   1   2   3   4   5
Comments: _____

Notes for Next time:

Comments/ Thoughts post-cook:

Barbecue Log Book

Date: [_____]

Meat Type:_____
☐Poultry ☐Pork ☐Beef ☐Seafood ☐Other
Comments:

Weight:_____
Price/lb:_____
☐Fresh ☐Frozen
Brand/ Store:_____

Meat preparation:

Rub:_____
_____

Glaze:_____
_____

Marinade:_____
_____

Mop Sauce:_____
_____

Cooking procedure:

Cooker used:

Weather/ Conditions:

Target Cooker Temp:_____
Target Wrap Temp:_____
Final Meat Temp:_____
Rest Time length:_____

Fuel used:_____
Qty used:_____

Est Cook Length:_____
Time on:_____ Time off:_____
Actual Cook Length:_____

Wood used:_____
Qty used:_____
☐Logs ☐Chunks ☐Chips
☐Dry ☐Soaked

Comments/ Notes for pre-cook:

Cook Notes:

Post Cook

Date:_____

Post-Cook Evaluation
Rank 1-5 with 5 being Heavenly Perfection, and 1
being Burnt to a Crisp! This allows you to track your cooks.

Exterior Appearance................. 1   2   3   4   5
Comments:_____

Bark Quality............................ 1   2   3   4   5
Comments: _____

Smoke Ring............................. 1   2   3   4   5
Comments: _____

Overall Tenderness.................. 1   2   3   4   5
Comments: _____

Moisture.................................. 1   2   3   4   5
Comments: _____

Aroma..................................... 1   2   3   4   5
Comments: _____

Flavor...................................... 1   2   3   4   5
Comments: _____

Other:_____ 1   2   3   4   5
Comments: _____

Notes for Next time:

Comments/ Thoughts post-cook:

Barbecue Log Book

Date: _____

Meat Type:_____
☐Poultry ☐Pork ☐Beef ☐Seafood ☐Other
Comments:

Weight:_____
Price/lb:_____
☐Fresh ☐Frozen
Brand/ Store:_____

Meat preparation:

Rub:_____

Glaze:_____

Marinade:_____

Mop Sauce:_____

Cooking procedure:

Cooker used:

Weather/ Conditions:

Target Cooker Temp:_____
Target Wrap Temp:_____
Final Meat Temp:_____
Rest Time length:_____

Fuel used:_____
Qty used:_____

Est Cook Length:_____
Time on:_____ Time off:_____
Actual Cook Length:_____

Wood used:_____
Qty used:_____
☐Logs ☐Chunks ☐Chips
☐Dry ☐Soaked

Comments/ Notes for pre-cook:

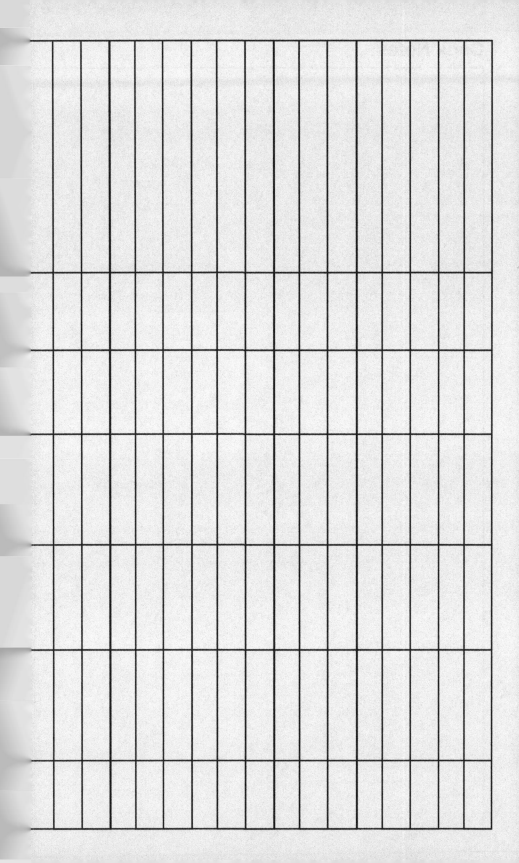

Cook Notes:

Post Cook

Date:_____

Post-Cook Evaluation
Rank 1-5 with 5 being Heavenly Perfection, and 1
being Burnt to a Crisp! This allows you to track your cooks.

Exterior Appearance................   1   2   3   4   5
Comments:_____

Bark Quality...........................   1   2   3   4   5
Comments: _____

Smoke Ring...........................   1   2   3   4   5
Comments: _____

Overall Tenderness..................   1   2   3   4   5
Comments: _____

Moisture.................................   1   2   3   4   5
Comments: _____

Aroma.....................................   1   2   3   4   5
Comments: _____

Flavor.....................................   1   2   3   4   5
Comments: _____

Other:_____   1   2   3   4   5
Comments: _____

Notes for Next time:

Comments/ Thoughts post-cook:

Barbecue Log Book

Date: _____

Meat Type:_____
☐Poultry ☐Pork ☐Beef ☐Seafood ☐Other
Comments:

Weight:_____
Price/lb:_____
☐Fresh ☐Frozen
Brand/ Store:_____

Meat preparation:

Rub:_____

Glaze:_____

Marinade:_____

Mop Sauce:_____

Cooking procedure:

Cooker used:

Weather/ Conditions:

Target Cooker Temp:_____
Target Wrap Temp:_____
Final Meat Temp:_____
Rest Time length:_____

Fuel used:_____
Qty used:_____

Est Cook Length:_____
Time on:_____ Time off:_____
Actual Cook Length:_____

Wood used:_____
Qty used:_____
☐Logs ☐Chunks ☐Chips
☐Dry ☐Soaked

Comments/ Notes for pre-cook:

Cook Notes:

Post Cook

Date:_____

Post-Cook Evaluation
Rank 1-5 with 5 being Heavenly Perfection, and 1
being Burnt to a Crisp! This allows you to track your cooks.

Exterior Appearance...............   1   2   3   4   5
Comments:_____

Bark Quality...........................   1   2   3   4   5
Comments: _____

Smoke Ring............................   1   2   3   4   5
Comments: _____

Overall Tenderness.................   1   2   3   4   5
Comments: _____

Moisture..................................   1   2   3   4   5
Comments: _____

Aroma.....................................   1   2   3   4   5
Comments: _____

Flavor......................................   1   2   3   4   5
Comments: _____

Other:_____   1   2   3   4   5
Comments: _____

Notes for Next time:

Comments/ Thoughts post-cook:

Barbecue Log Book

Date: _____

Meat Type:_____
☐Poultry ☐Pork ☐Beef ☐Seafood ☐Other
Comments:

Weight:_____
Price/lb:_____
☐Fresh ☐Frozen
Brand/ Store:_____

Meat preparation:

Rub:_____

Glaze:_____

Marinade:_____

Mop Sauce:_____

Cooking procedure:

Cooker used:

Weather/ Conditions:

Target Cooker Temp:_____
Target Wrap Temp:_____
Final Meat Temp:_____
Rest Time length:_____

Fuel used:_____
Qty used:_____

Est Cook Length:_____
Time on:_____ Time off:_____
Actual Cook Length:_____

Wood used:_____
Qty used:_____
☐Logs ☐Chunks ☐Chips
☐Dry ☐Soaked

Comments/ Notes for pre-cook:

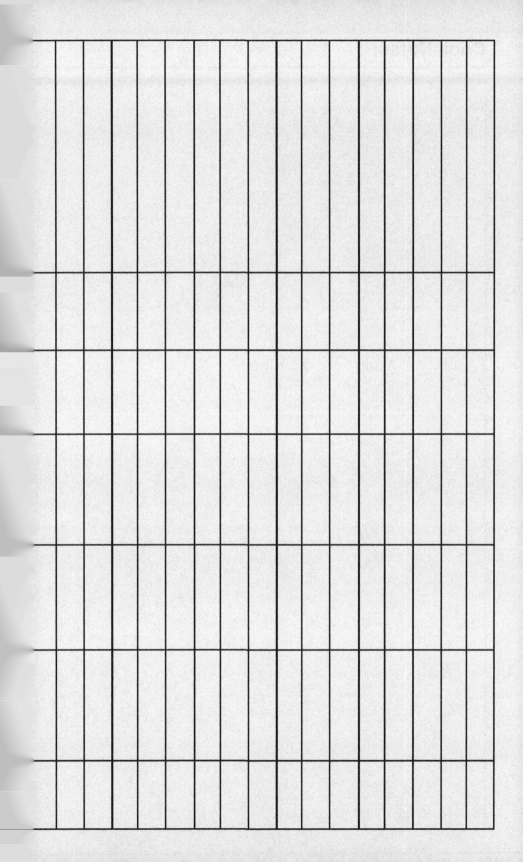

Cook Notes:

Post Cook

Date:_____

Exterior Appearance.................   1   2   3   4   5
Comments:_____

Bark Quality............................   1   2   3   4   5
Comments: _____

Smoke Ring............................   1   2   3   4   5
Comments: _____

Overall Tenderness.................   1   2   3   4   5
Comments: _____

Moisture...................................   1   2   3   4   5
Comments: _____

Aroma......................................   1   2   3   4   5
Comments: _____

Flavor......................................   1   2   3   4   5
Comments: _____

Other:_____   1   2   3   4   5
Comments: _____

Notes for Next time:

Comments/ Thoughts post-cook:

Barbecue Log Book

Date: [   ]

Meat Type:_____
☐Poultry ☐Pork ☐Beef ☐Seafood ☐Other
Comments:

Weight:_____
Price/lb:_____
☐Fresh ☐Frozen
Brand/ Store:_____

Meat preparation:

Rub:_____

Glaze:_____

Marinade:_____

Mop Sauce:_____

Cooking procedure:

Cooker used:

Weather/ Conditions:

Target Cooker Temp:_____
Target Wrap Temp:_____
Final Meat Temp:_____
Rest Time length:_____

Fuel used:_____
Qty used:_____

Est Cook Length:_____
Time on:_____ Time off:_____
Actual Cook Length:_____

Wood used:_____
Qty used:_____
☐Logs ☐Chunks ☐Chips
☐Dry ☐Soaked

Comments/ Notes for pre-cook:

Cook Notes:

Post Cook

Date:_____

Post-Cook Evaluation
Rank 1-5 with 5 being Heavenly Perfection, and 1
being Burnt to a Crisp! This allows you to track your cooks.

Exterior Appearance................ 1   2   3   4   5
Comments:_____

Bark Quality............................ 1   2   3   4   5
Comments: _____

Smoke Ring............................. 1   2   3   4   5
Comments: _____

Overall Tenderness.................. 1   2   3   4   5
Comments: _____

Moisture.................................. 1   2   3   4   5
Comments: _____

Aroma..................................... 1   2   3   4   5
Comments: _____

Flavor..................................... 1   2   3   4   5
Comments: _____

Other:_____ 1   2   3   4   5
Comments: _____

Notes for Next time:

Comments/ Thoughts post-cook:

Barbecue Log Book

Date: [   ]

Meat Type:_____
☐Poultry ☐Pork ☐Beef ☐Seafood ☐Other
Comments:

Weight:_____
Price/lb:_____
☐Fresh ☐Frozen
Brand/ Store:_____

Meat preparation:

Rub:_____

Glaze:_____

Marinade:_____

Mop Sauce:_____

Cooking procedure:

Cooker used:

Weather/ Conditions:

Target Cooker Temp:_____
Target Wrap Temp:_____
Final Meat Temp:_____
Rest Time length:_____

Fuel used:_____
Qty used:_____

Est Cook Length:_____
Time on:_____ Time off:_____
Actual Cook Length:_____

Wood used:_____
Qty used:_____
☐Logs ☐Chunks ☐Chips
☐Dry ☐Soaked

Comments/ Notes for pre-cook:

Cook Notes:

Post Cook

Date:_____

Post-Cook Evaluation
Rank 1-5 with 5 being Heavenly Perfection, and 1
being Burnt to a Crisp! This allows you to track your cooks.

Exterior Appearance................   1   2   3   4   5
Comments:_____

Bark Quality............................   1   2   3   4   5
Comments: _____

Smoke Ring............................   1   2   3   4   5
Comments: _____

Overall Tenderness.................   1   2   3   4   5
Comments: _____

Moisture..................................   1   2   3   4   5
Comments: _____

Aroma.....................................   1   2   3   4   5
Comments: _____

Flavor.....................................   1   2   3   4   5
Comments: _____

Other:_____   1   2   3   4   5
Comments: _____

Notes for Next time:

Comments/ Thoughts post-cook:

Barbecue Log Book

Date: [   ]

Meat Type:_____
☐Poultry ☐Pork ☐Beef ☐Seafood ☐Other
Comments:

Weight:_____
Price/lb:_____
☐Fresh ☐Frozen
Brand/ Store:_____

Meat preparation:

Rub:_____

Glaze:_____

Marinade:_____

Mop Sauce:_____

Cooking procedure:

Cooker used:

Weather/ Conditions:

Target Cooker Temp:_____
Target Wrap Temp:_____
Final Meat Temp:_____
Rest Time length:_____

Fuel used:_____
Qty used:_____

Est Cook Length:_____
Time on:_____ Time off:_____
Actual Cook Length:_____

Wood used:_____
Qty used:_____
☐Logs ☐Chunks ☐Chips
☐Dry ☐Soaked

Comments/ Notes for pre-cook:

Cook Notes:

Post Cook

Date:_____

Post-Cook Evaluation
Rank 1-5 with 5 being Heavenly Perfection, and 1
being Burnt to a Crisp! This allows you to track your cooks.

Exterior Appearance................. 1   2   3   4   5
Comments:_____

Bark Quality............................ 1   2   3   4   5
Comments: _____

Smoke Ring............................. 1   2   3   4   5
Comments: _____

Overall Tenderness.................. 1   2   3   4   5
Comments: _____

Moisture.................................. 1   2   3   4   5
Comments: _____

Aroma..................................... 1   2   3   4   5
Comments: _____

Flavor...................................... 1   2   3   4   5
Comments: _____

Other:_____ 1   2   3   4   5
Comments: _____

Notes for Next time:

Comments/ Thoughts post-cook:

Barbecue Log Book

Date: [   ]

Meat Type:_____
☐Poultry ☐Pork ☐Beef ☐Seafood ☐Other
Comments:

Weight:_____
Price/lb:_____
☐Fresh ☐ Frozen
Brand/ Store:_____

Meat preparation:

Rub:_____

Glaze:_____

Marinade:_____

Mop Sauce:_____

Cooking procedure:

Cooker used:

Weather/ Conditions:

Target Cooker Temp:_____
Target Wrap Temp:_____
Final Meat Temp:_____
Rest Time length:_____

Est Cook Length:_____
Time on:_____ Time off:_____
Actual Cook Length:_____

Fuel used:_____
Qty used:_____

Wood used:_____
Qty used:_____
☐Logs ☐Chunks ☐Chips
☐Dry ☐Soaked

Comments/ Notes for pre-cook:

Cook Notes:

Post Cook

Date:_____

Post-Cook Evaluation
Rank 1-5 with 5 being Heavenly Perfection, and 1
being Burnt to a Crisp! This allows you to track your cooks.

Exterior Appearance................ 1   2   3   4   5
Comments:_____

Bark Quality........................... 1   2   3   4   5
Comments: _____

Smoke Ring............................ 1   2   3   4   5
Comments: _____

Overall Tenderness................. 1   2   3   4   5
Comments: _____

Moisture................................. 1   2   3   4   5
Comments: _____

Aroma.................................... 1   2   3   4   5
Comments: _____

Flavor.................................... 1   2   3   4   5
Comments: _____

Other:_____ 1   2   3   4   5
Comments: _____

Notes for Next time:

Comments/ Thoughts post-cook:

Barbecue Log Book

Date: [_____]

Meat Type:_____
☐Poultry ☐Pork ☐Beef ☐Seafood ☐Other
Comments:

Weight:_____
Price/lb:_____
☐Fresh ☐Frozen
Brand/ Store:_____

Meat preparation:

Rub:_____

Glaze:_____

Marinade:_____

Mop Sauce:_____

Cooking procedure:

Cooker used:

Weather/ Conditions:

Target Cooker Temp:_____
Target Wrap Temp:_____
Final Meat Temp:_____
Rest Time length:_____

Fuel used:_____
Qty used:_____

Est Cook Length:_____
Time on:_____ Time off:_____
Actual Cook Length:_____

Wood used:_____
Qty used:_____
☐Logs ☐Chunks ☐Chips
☐Dry ☐Soaked

Comments/ Notes for pre-cook:

Cook Notes:

Post Cook

Date:_____

Exterior Appearance.................   1   2   3   4   5
Comments:_____

Bark Quality............................   1   2   3   4   5
Comments: _____

Smoke Ring............................   1   2   3   4   5
Comments: _____

Overall Tenderness.................   1   2   3   4   5
Comments: _____

Moisture..................................   1   2   3   4   5
Comments: _____

Aroma....................................   1   2   3   4   5
Comments: _____

Flavor.....................................   1   2   3   4   5
Comments: _____

Other:_____   1   2   3   4   5
Comments: _____

Notes for Next time:

Comments/ Thoughts post-cook:

Barbecue Log Book

Date: _____

Meat Type:_____
☐Poultry ☐Pork ☐Beef ☐Seafood ☐Other
Comments:

Weight:_____
Price/lb:_____
☐Fresh ☐ Frozen
Brand/ Store:_____

Meat preparation:

Rub:_____

Glaze:_____

Marinade:_____

Mop Sauce:_____

Cooking procedure:

Cooker used:

Weather/ Conditions:

Target Cooker Temp:_____
Target Wrap Temp:_____
Final Meat Temp:_____
Rest Time length:_____

Fuel used:_____
Qty used:_____

Est Cook Length:_____
Time on:_____ Time off:_____
Actual Cook Length:_____

Wood used:_____
Qty used:_____
☐Logs ☐Chunks ☐Chips
☐Dry ☐Soaked

Comments/ Notes for pre-cook:

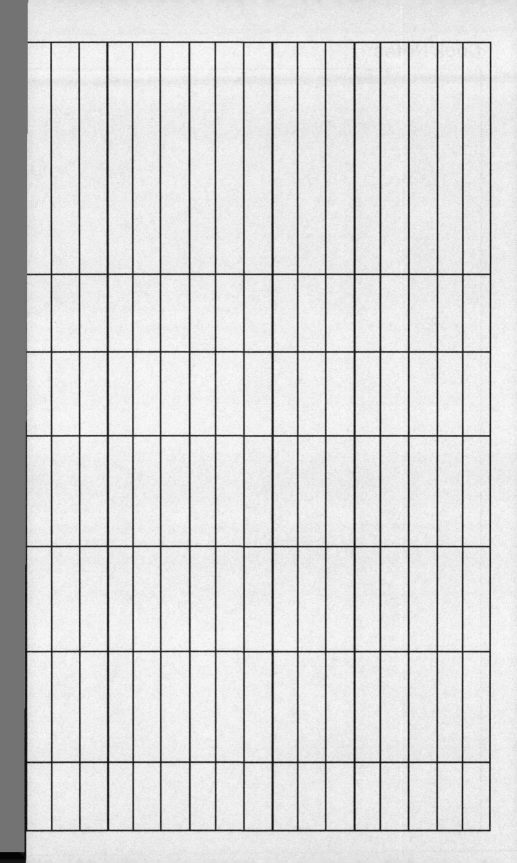

Cook Notes:

Post Cook

Date:_____

Exterior Appearance.................   1   2   3   4   5
Comments:_____

Bark Quality............................   1   2   3   4   5
Comments: _____

Smoke Ring.............................   1   2   3   4   5
Comments: _____

Overall Tenderness..................   1   2   3   4   5
Comments: _____

Moisture..................................   1   2   3   4   5
Comments: _____

Aroma.....................................   1   2   3   4   5
Comments: _____

Flavor......................................   1   2   3   4   5
Comments: _____

Other:_____   1   2   3   4   5
Comments: _____

Notes for Next time:

Comments/ Thoughts post-cook:

Barbecue Log Book

Date: [_____]

Meat Type:_____
☐Poultry ☐Pork ☐Beef ☐Seafood ☐Other
Comments:

Weight:_____
Price/lb:_____
☐Fresh ☐ Frozen
Brand/ Store:_____

Meat preparation:

Rub:_____

Glaze:_____

Marinade:_____

Mop Sauce:_____

Cooking procedure:

Cooker used:

Weather/ Conditions:

Target Cooker Temp:_____
Target Wrap Temp:_____
Final Meat Temp:_____
Rest Time length:_____

Fuel used:_____
Qty used:_____

Est Cook Length:_____
Time on:_____ Time off:_____
Actual Cook Length:_____

Wood used:_____
Qty used:_____
☐Logs ☐Chunks ☐Chips
☐Dry ☐Soaked

Comments/ Notes for pre-cook:

Cook Notes:

Post Cook

Date:_____

Post-Cook Evaluation
Rank 1-5 with 5 being Heavenly Perfection, and 1
being Burnt to a Crisp! This allows you to track your cooks.

Exterior Appearance.................   1   2   3   4   5
Comments:_____

Bark Quality............................   1   2   3   4   5
Comments: _____

Smoke Ring.............................   1   2   3   4   5
Comments: _____

Overall Tenderness..................   1   2   3   4   5
Comments: _____

Moisture..................................   1   2   3   4   5
Comments: _____

Aroma.....................................   1   2   3   4   5
Comments: _____

Flavor.....................................   1   2   3   4   5
Comments: _____

Other:_____   1   2   3   4   5
Comments: _____

Notes for Next time:

Comments/ Thoughts post-cook:

Barbecue Log Book

Date: [_____]

Meat Type:_____
☐Poultry ☐Pork ☐Beef ☐Seafood ☐Other
Comments:

Weight:_____
Price/lb:_____
☐Fresh ☐Frozen
Brand/ Store:_____

Meat preparation:

Rub:_____

Glaze:_____

Marinade:_____

Mop Sauce:_____

Cooking procedure:

Cooker used:

Weather/ Conditions:

Target Cooker Temp:_____
Target Wrap Temp:_____
Final Meat Temp:_____
Rest Time length:_____

Fuel used:_____
Qty used:_____

Est Cook Length:_____
Time on:_____ Time off:_____
Actual Cook Length:_____

Wood used:_____
Qty used:_____
☐Logs ☐Chunks ☐Chips
☐Dry ☐Soaked

Comments/ Notes for pre-cook:

Cook Notes:

Post Cook

Date:_____

Post-Cook Evaluation
Rank 1-5 with 5 being Heavenly Perfection, and 1
being Burnt to a Crisp! This allows you to track your cooks.

Exterior Appearance................   1   2   3   4   5
Comments:_____

Bark Quality...........................   1   2   3   4   5
Comments: _____

Smoke Ring............................   1   2   3   4   5
Comments: _____

Overall Tenderness..................   1   2   3   4   5
Comments: _____

Moisture.................................   1   2   3   4   5
Comments: _____

Aroma....................................   1   2   3   4   5
Comments: _____

Flavor.....................................   1   2   3   4   5
Comments: _____

Other:_____   1   2   3   4   5
Comments: _____

Notes for Next time:

Comments/ Thoughts post-cook:

Barbecue Log Book

Date: [_____]

Meat Type:_____
☐Poultry ☐Pork ☐Beef ☐Seafood ☐Other
Comments:

Weight:_____
Price/lb:_____
☐Fresh ☐ Frozen
Brand/ Store:_____

Meat preparation:

Rub:_____
_____

Glaze:_____
_____

Marinade:_____
_____

Mop Sauce:_____
_____

Cooking procedure:

Cooker used:

Weather/ Conditions:

Target Cooker Temp:_____
Target Wrap Temp:_____
Final Meat Temp:_____
Rest Time length:_____

Fuel used:_____
Qty used:_____

Est Cook Length:_____
Time on:_____ Time off:_____
Actual Cook Length:_____

Wood used:_____
Qty used:_____
☐Logs ☐Chunks ☐Chips
☐Dry ☐Soaked

Comments/ Notes for pre-cook:

Cook Notes:

Post Cook

Date:_____

Post-Cook Evaluation
Rank 1-5 with 5 being Heavenly Perfection, and 1
being Burnt to a Crisp! This allows you to track your cooks.

Exterior Appearance................ 1   2   3   4   5
Comments:_____

Bark Quality............................ 1   2   3   4   5
Comments: _____

Smoke Ring............................. 1   2   3   4   5
Comments: _____

Overall Tenderness................. 1   2   3   4   5
Comments: _____

Moisture................................. 1   2   3   4   5
Comments: _____

Aroma.................................... 1   2   3   4   5
Comments: _____

Flavor.................................... 1   2   3   4   5
Comments: _____

Other:_____ 1   2   3   4   5
Comments: _____

Notes for Next time:

Comments/ Thoughts post-cook:

Barbecue Log Book

Date: [   ]

Meat Type:_____
☐Poultry ☐Pork ☐Beef ☐Seafood ☐Other
Comments:

Weight:_____
Price/lb:_____
☐Fresh ☐Frozen
Brand/ Store:_____

Meat preparation:

Rub:_____

Glaze:_____

Marinade:_____

Mop Sauce:_____

Cooking procedure:

Cooker used:

Weather/ Conditions:

Target Cooker Temp:_____
Target Wrap Temp:_____
Final Meat Temp:_____
Rest Time length:_____

Fuel used:_____
Qty used:_____

Est Cook Length:_____
Time on:_____ Time off:_____
Actual Cook Length:_____

Wood used:_____
Qty used:_____
☐Logs ☐Chunks ☐Chips
☐Dry ☐Soaked

Comments/ Notes for pre-cook:

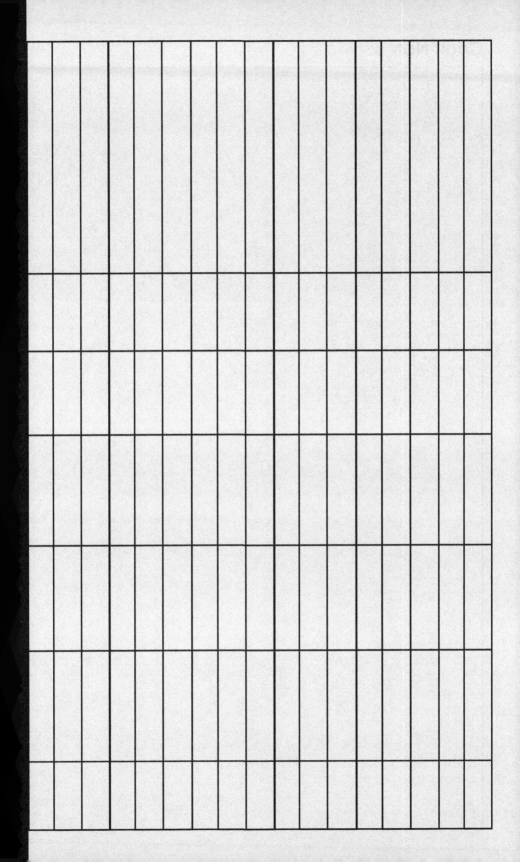

Cook Notes:

Post Cook

Date:_____

Post-Cook Evaluation
Rank 1-5 with 5 being Heavenly Perfection, and 1
being Burnt to a Crisp! This allows you to track your cooks.

Exterior Appearance................ 1   2   3   4   5
Comments:_____

Bark Quality............................ 1   2   3   4   5
Comments: _____

Smoke Ring............................ 1   2   3   4   5
Comments: _____

Overall Tenderness................. 1   2   3   4   5
Comments: _____

Moisture.................................. 1   2   3   4   5
Comments: _____

Aroma..................................... 1   2   3   4   5
Comments: _____

Flavor..................................... 1   2   3   4   5
Comments: _____

Other:_____ 1   2   3   4   5
Comments: _____

Notes for Next time:

Comments/ Thoughts post-cook:

Barbecue Log Book

Date: _____

Meat Type:_____
☐Poultry ☐Pork ☐Beef ☐Seafood ☐Other
Comments:

Weight:_____
Price/lb:_____
☐Fresh ☐Frozen
Brand/ Store:_____

Meat preparation:

Rub:_____

Glaze:_____

Marinade:_____

Mop Sauce:_____

Cooking procedure:

Cooker used:

Weather/ Conditions:

Target Cooker Temp:_____
Target Wrap Temp:_____
Final Meat Temp:_____
Rest Time length:_____

Fuel used:_____
Qty used:_____

Est Cook Length:_____
Time on:_____ Time off:_____
Actual Cook Length:_____

Wood used:_____
Qty used:_____
☐Logs ☐Chunks ☐Chips
☐Dry ☐Soaked

Comments/ Notes for pre-cook:

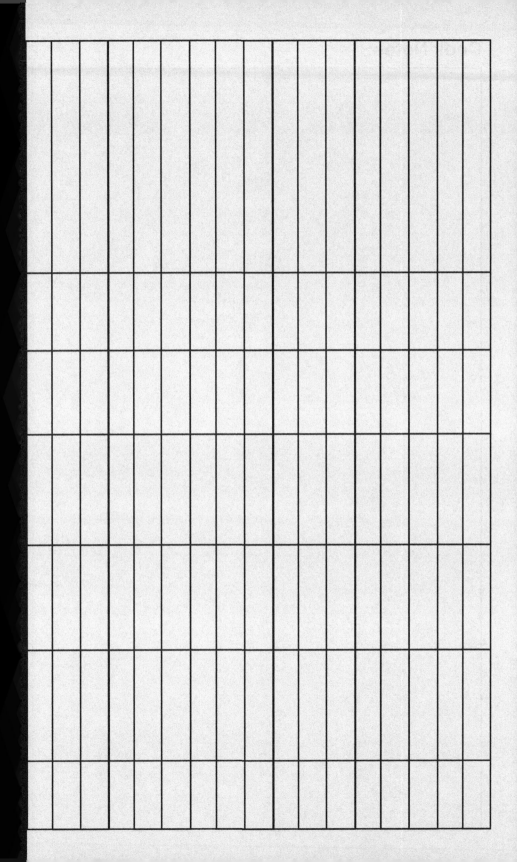

Cook Notes:

Post Cook

Date:_____

Post-Cook Evaluation
Rank 1-5 with 5 being Heavenly Perfection, and 1
being Burnt to a Crisp! This allows you to track your cooks.

Exterior Appearance................. 1   2   3   4   5
Comments:_____

Bark Quality............................ 1   2   3   4   5
Comments: _____

Smoke Ring............................. 1   2   3   4   5
Comments: _____

Overall Tenderness.................. 1   2   3   4   5
Comments: _____

Moisture.................................. 1   2   3   4   5
Comments: _____

Aroma..................................... 1   2   3   4   5
Comments: _____

Flavor..................................... 1   2   3   4   5
Comments: _____

Other:_____ 1   2   3   4   5
Comments: _____

Notes for Next time:

Comments/ Thoughts post-cook:

Barbecue Log Book

Date: _____

Meat Type:_____
☐Poultry ☐Pork ☐Beef ☐Seafood ☐Other
Comments:

Weight:_____
Price/lb:_____
☐ Fresh ☐ Frozen
Brand/ Store:_____

Meat preparation:

Rub:_____

Glaze:_____
_____

_____

Marinade:_____

Mop Sauce:_____
_____

_____

Cooking procedure:

Cooker used:

Weather/ Conditions:

Target Cooker Temp:_____
Target Wrap Temp:_____
Final Meat Temp:_____
Rest Time length:_____

Est Cook Length:_____
Time on:_____ Time off:_____
Actual Cook Length:_____

Fuel used:_____
Qty used:_____

Wood used:_____
Qty used:_____
  ☐Logs ☐Chunks ☐Chips
  ☐Dry ☐Soaked

Comments/ Notes for pre-cook:

Cook Notes:

Post Cook

Date:_____

Post-Cook Evaluation
Rank 1-5 with 5 being Heavenly Perfection, and 1
being Burnt to a Crisp! This allows you to track your cooks.

Exterior Appearance.................   1   2   3   4   5
Comments:_____

Bark Quality............................   1   2   3   4   5
Comments: _____

Smoke Ring.............................   1   2   3   4   5
Comments: _____

Overall Tenderness.................   1   2   3   4   5
Comments: _____

Moisture..................................   1   2   3   4   5
Comments: _____

Aroma.....................................   1   2   3   4   5
Comments: _____

Flavor......................................   1   2   3   4   5
Comments: _____

Other:_____   1   2   3   4   5
Comments: _____

Notes for Next time:

Comments/ Thoughts post-cook:

Barbecue Log Book

Date: _____

Meat Type:_____
☐Poultry ☐Pork ☐Beef ☐Seafood ☐Other
Comments:

Weight:_____
Price/lb:_____
☐Fresh ☐Frozen
Brand/ Store:_____

Meat preparation:

Rub:_____

Glaze:_____
_____

Marinade:_____
_____

Mop Sauce:_____
_____

Cooking procedure:

Cooker used:

Weather/ Conditions:

Target Cooker Temp:_____
Target Wrap Temp:_____
Final Meat Temp:_____
Rest Time length:_____

Fuel used:_____
Qty used:_____

Est Cook Length:_____
Time on:_____ Time off:_____
Actual Cook Length:_____

Wood used:_____
Qty used:_____
☐Logs ☐Chunks ☐Chips
☐Dry ☐Soaked

Comments/ Notes for pre-cook:

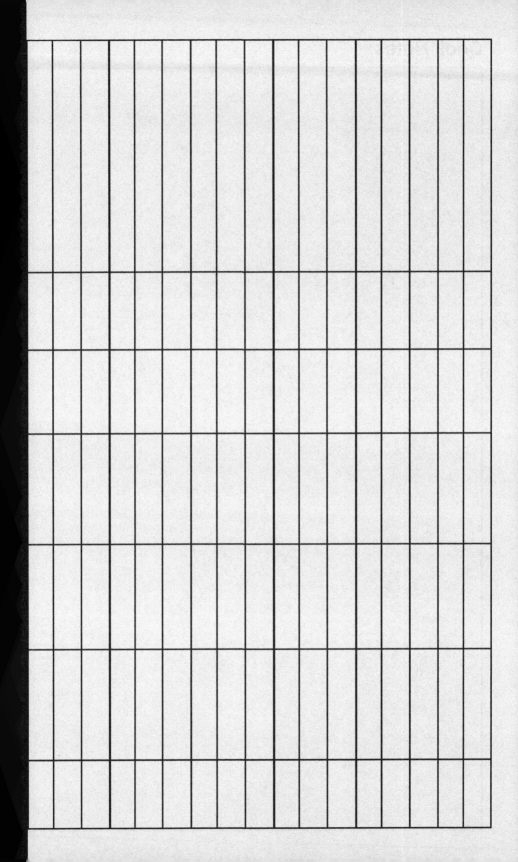

Cook Notes:

Post Cook

Date:_____

Exterior Appearance................   1   2   3   4   5
Comments:_____

Bark Quality............................   1   2   3   4   5
Comments: _____

Smoke Ring............................   1   2   3   4   5
Comments: _____

Overall Tenderness..................   1   2   3   4   5
Comments: _____

Moisture..................................   1   2   3   4   5
Comments: _____

Aroma.....................................   1   2   3   4   5
Comments: _____

Flavor.....................................   1   2   3   4   5
Comments: _____

Other:_____   1   2   3   4   5
Comments: _____

Notes for Next time:

Comments/ Thoughts post-cook:

Barbecue Log Book

Date: _____

Meat Type:_____
☐Poultry ☐Pork ☐Beef ☐Seafood ☐Other
Comments:

Weight:_____
Price/lb:_____
☐Fresh   ☐ Frozen
Brand/ Store:_____

Meat preparation:

Rub:_____

Glaze:_____
_____

Marinade:_____
_____

Mop Sauce:_____
_____

Cooking procedure:

Cooker used:

Weather/ Conditions:

Target Cooker Temp:_____
Target Wrap Temp:_____
Final Meat Temp:_____
Rest Time length:_____

Fuel used:_____
Qty used:_____

Est Cook Length:_____
Time on:_____ Time off:_____
Actual Cook Length:_____

Wood used:_____
Qty used:_____
☐Logs ☐Chunks ☐Chips
☐Dry ☐Soaked

Comments/ Notes for pre-cook:

Cook Notes:

Post Cook

Date:_____

Post-Cook Evaluation
Rank 1-5 with 5 being Heavenly Perfection, and 1
being Burnt to a Crisp! This allows you to track your cooks.

Exterior Appearance.................   1   2   3   4   5
Comments:_____

Bark Quality............................   1   2   3   4   5
Comments: _____

Smoke Ring.............................   1   2   3   4   5
Comments: _____

Overall Tenderness..................   1   2   3   4   5
Comments: _____

Moisture..................................   1   2   3   4   5
Comments: _____

Aroma.....................................   1   2   3   4   5
Comments: _____

Flavor.....................................   1   2   3   4   5
Comments: _____

Other:_____   1   2   3   4   5
Comments: _____

Notes for Next time:

Comments/ Thoughts post-cook:

Barbecue Log Book

Date: _____

Meat Type:_____
☐Poultry ☐Pork ☐Beef ☐Seafood ☐Other
Comments:

Weight:_____
Price/lb:_____
☐Fresh ☐ Frozen
Brand/ Store:_____

Meat preparation:

Rub:_____

Glaze:_____

Marinade:_____

Mop Sauce:_____

Cooking procedure:

Cooker used:

Weather/ Conditions:

Target Cooker Temp:_____
Target Wrap Temp:_____
Final Meat Temp:_____
Rest Time length:_____

Fuel used:_____
Qty used:_____

Est Cook Length:_____
Time on:_____ Time off:_____
Actual Cook Length:_____

Wood used:_____
Qty used:_____
☐Logs ☐Chunks ☐Chips
☐Dry ☐Soaked

Comments/ Notes for pre-cook:

Cook Notes:

Post Cook

Date:_____

Post-Cook Evaluation
Rank 1-5 with 5 being Heavenly Perfection, and 1
being Burnt to a Crisp! This allows you to track your cooks.

Exterior Appearance................   1   2   3   4   5
Comments:_____

Bark Quality...........................   1   2   3   4   5
Comments: _____

Smoke Ring...........................   1   2   3   4   5
Comments: _____

Overall Tenderness.................   1   2   3   4   5
Comments: _____

Moisture.................................   1   2   3   4   5
Comments: _____

Aroma....................................   1   2   3   4   5
Comments: _____

Flavor.....................................   1   2   3   4   5
Comments: _____

Other:_____   1   2   3   4   5
Comments: _____

Notes for Next time:

Comments/ Thoughts post-cook:

Barbecue Log Book

Date: _____

Meat Type:_____
☐Poultry ☐Pork ☐Beef ☐Seafood ☐Other
Comments:

Weight:_____
Price/lb:_____
☐Fresh   ☐Frozen
Brand/ Store:_____

Meat preparation:

Rub:_____

Glaze:_____

Marinade:_____

Mop Sauce:_____

Cooking procedure:

Cooker used:

Weather/ Conditions:

Target Cooker Temp:_____
Target Wrap Temp:_____
Final Meat Temp:_____
Rest Time length:_____

Fuel used:_____
Qty used:_____

Est Cook Length:_____
Time on:_____ Time off:_____
Actual Cook Length:_____

Wood used:_____
Qty used:_____
  ☐Logs ☐Chunks ☐Chips
  ☐Dry ☐Soaked

Comments/ Notes for pre-cook:

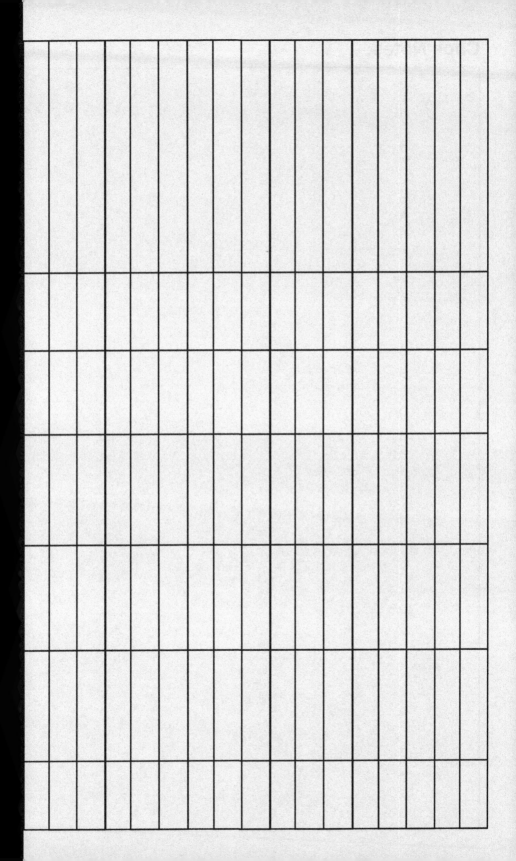

Cook Notes:

Post Cook

Date:_____

Post-Cook Evaluation
Rank 1-5 with 5 being Heavenly Perfection, and 1
being Burnt to a Crisp! This allows you to track your cooks.

Exterior Appearance................   1   2   3   4   5
Comments:_____

Bark Quality............................   1   2   3   4   5
Comments: _____

Smoke Ring............................   1   2   3   4   5
Comments: _____

Overall Tenderness..................   1   2   3   4   5
Comments: _____

Moisture..................................   1   2   3   4   5
Comments: _____

Aroma.....................................:..   1   2   3   4   5
Comments: _____

Flavor......................................   1   2   3   4   5
Comments: _____

Other:_____   1   2   3   4   5
Comments: _____

Notes for Next time:

Comments/ Thoughts post-cook:

What is the Best Wood for Smoking Meat?

Oak
Oak is the quintessential go-to for smoking meat. It is a great place to start if you are a newbie to smoking. It will lend a medium to a strong flavor that is seldom overpowering.
Best Meat to Smoke Lamb, beef, brisket, and sausages

Hickory
The most versatile choice as it can be used to smoke wood in many ways. Be careful, though, because too much hickory flavor will cause your meat to have a more bitter flavor. It has a sweet, savory, and hearty, a bit bacony.
Best Meat to Smoke Larger cuts of ribs and pork shoulders, as well as almost all red meat and poultry.

Mesquite
A hardy wood packing intense flavor. It is recommended for grilling, or to be used in smaller quantities. It is famous for its strong, intense, and unique.
Best Meat to Smoke Red Meat and for adding additional flavor when grilling

Apple
Applewood is mild and sweet, lending a mellow flavor. Apple smoke flavors take a while to permeate the meat, so anticipate several hours of smoking.
Best Meat to Smoke Chicken, wild foul, pork

Pecan
Pecan will lend a rich, sweet, nutty flavor. In fact, the wood is so sweet that you may want to use a combination of it with another harder wood to balance out the flavor.
Best Meat to Smoke Briskets, roasts, and ribs

Cherry
Cherry is mild and fruity, and when mixed with other hardwood like hickory, the two flavors compliment each other for an amazing result.
Best Meat to Smoke Chicken, turkey, ham

Maple
One of the most subtle smoking wood, it will impart a more subtle smoke flavor. Use maple for a sweet, light, mild smokiness.
Best Meat to Smoke Poultry, pork, game foul

Alder
A very light and sweet flavor profile. It lends a delicate and sweet characteristic.
Best Meat to Smoke Fish, like salmon and other Pacific Northwestern types

Pork and beef ribs, pork shoulders, and beef brisket.
These cuts are safe at 145°F, but we deliberately cook these meats up to 203°F, well past well done, in order to melt the connective tissues that are rife in these tough cuts.

Ground meat, burgers, and sausage.
The USDA recommended temp is 160°F and it should be adhered to closely.

Poultry.
Serve poultry at 165°F and remove it at no lower than 160°F allowing for 5°F carryover.

Fish.
USDA recommends serving it at 145°F. It is easy to overcook fish, so be vigilant.

Rare 125F
Med Rare 135F
Medium 145F
Med Well 155F
Burnt 160F
Brisket 205F

145F
Pulled 205F

Rare 125F
Med Rare 140F
Medium 150F
Med Well 165F
Well 175F

165F

145F

Made in United States
Orlando, FL
15 June 2023

34181847R00115